For Noah and Nico,
Southampton's future strikeforce

Matt Oldfield is an accomplished writer and the editor-in-chief of football review site *Of Pitch & Page*. Tom Oldfield is a freelance sports writer and the author of biographies on Cristiano Ronaldo, Arsène Wenger and Rafael Nadal.

Cover illustration by Dan Leydon.
To learn more about Dan visit danleydon.com
To purchase his artwork visit etsy.com/shop/footynews
Or just follow him on Twitter @danleydon

TABLE OF CONTENTS

CHAPTER 1 – **A DRAMATIC GOODBYE** 7

CHAPTER 2 – **LA CASTELLANE** 13

CHAPTER 3 – **THE PLACE DE LA TARTANE** 19

CHAPTER 4 – **TOURNAMENT FOOTBALL** 26

CHAPTER 5 – **FRANCE VS ALGERIA** 32

CHAPTER 6 – **SEPTÈMES** 38

CHAPTER 7 – **EURO 84: BEST BIRTHDAY EVER** 43

CHAPTER 8 – **SCOUTED** 50

CHAPTER 9 – **CALMING DOWN AT CANNES** 56

CHAPTER 10 – **ZINEDINE AND VÉRONIQUE** 61

CHAPTER 11 – **THE START OF GREAT THINGS** 67

CHAPTER 12 – **ZIZOU AT BORDEAUX** 73

CHAPTER 13 – **FIRST STEPS WITH FRANCE** 79

CHAPTER 14 – **EUROPEAN ADVENTURES** 85

CHAPTER 15 – **JOY AND DESPAIR AT JUVENTUS** 92

CHAPTER 16 – **WORLD CUP 1998: THE ROAD TO
ANOTHER FINAL** 100

CHAPTER 17 – **WORLD CUP 1998: THE FINAL** 108

CHAPTER 18 – **BACK DOWN TO EARTH** 114

CHAPTER 19 – **EURO 2000** 122

CHAPTER 20 – **READY FOR REAL MADRID** 128

CHAPTER 21 – **CHAMPIONS LEAGUE GLORY** 134

CHAPTER 22 – **THE GALÁCTICOS** 140

CHAPTER 23 – **WORLD CUP 2006** 151

CHAPTER 1

A DRAMATIC GOODBYE

Zinedine Zidane stood on the pitch in Berlin and looked around him. There were 70,000 supporters watching in the stadium – half were supporting Italy and half were supporting his beloved France. He could hear his nickname being chanted.

Zizou! Zizou! Zizou!

This was it – his final match. After 108 international matches and over 500 club games for AS Cannes, Bordeaux, Juventus and Real Madrid, Zinedine was retiring from football. It still didn't feel real.

'Are you sure about this?' Véronique, his wife, had been asking him for months. 'You're going to miss the beautiful game, nearly as much as the beautiful game will miss you!'

But Zinedine had made his decision and his final match would be very special indeed – the 2006 World Cup Final. In 1998, Zinedine had helped France to win their first ever World Cup by scoring two brilliant goals in the final against Brazil. Could he do it again, eight years later, against Italy? It would be the perfect way to say goodbye.

'Come on!' Zinedine shouted as the game kicked off. He was the captain of France, their experienced leader.

After seven minutes, Florent Malouda ran into the penalty area and a defender tripped him. Penalty!

There was only one person who would take the penalty – 'Zizou', the coolest player around. Zinedine looked up at the goal and then down at the ball. He knew what he was going to do and it was going to be sensational. As he ran up, the keeper dived early. Zinedine calmly chipped the ball straight down the middle of the goal. It crashed off the crossbar and bounced down over the goal-line.

Gooooooooooooooaaaaaaaaaallllllllllllllllllllll!!!!!!!!!!

Zinedine didn't show any emotion as he turned away, but inside he felt a rush of joy and relief. He had scored in another World Cup Final! The France fans were going wild, chanting for him again and again: *Zizou! Zizou! Zizou!*

Thierry Henry was the first teammate to give him a big hug. 'Wow, only you would have the confidence to try a Panenka in a World Cup Final!'

But ten minutes later, Italy were level thanks to Marco Materazzi's header. France needed more from their leader.

'Stay calm!' Zinedine called to his teammates. 'If we're patient and pass the ball around, we'll get more chances to score.'

But Andrea Pirlo and Gennaro Gattuso weren't giving him any time or space in midfield to create. In his prime, Zinedine could glide past players with a sudden flash of brilliance. But now, after a long, tough tournament, his legs felt tired and heavy. It was so frustrating.

'Keep going!' the manager, Raymond Domenech, shouted to him.

In extra time, Zinedine dribbled around three Italians, passed to right-back Willy Sagnol and then kept running towards the penalty area. The cross was accurate but Zinedine was still a long way from goal. Both of his goals in the 1998 World Cup Final had been brilliant headers – could he do it again? He used his neck muscles to flick the ball with as much power as he could. The ball flew through the air but the keeper jumped up and tipped it over the bar.

So close! Zinedine put his hands to his face – he had missed a golden chance to score the winner. He screamed out in anger. He needed to calm down but he didn't – and the Italian centre-back Marco Materazzi was pulling his shirt.

'Hey, get off me!' Zinedine shouted.

As he ran back to defend, Materazzi shouted rude words at him and Zinedine lost his temper. It used to happen a lot when he was a kid, but Jean Varraud at Cannes and Rolland Courbis at Bordeaux had coached him to ignore it when opponents insulted him.

This time, though, Zinedine couldn't control

himself. He turned around and pushed Materazzi in the chest with his head. As the defender fell to the floor, Zinedine knew that he was in big trouble. In vain, he tried to explain things to the referee, but he reached into his pocket – red card!

The French fans were shocked. Zinedine had let his temper ruin his final match. He had let everyone down: his teammates, his family, his entire country. He gave his captain's armband to Willy and walked slowly past the World Cup trophy and down the tunnel.

France lost on penalties. When they needed him most, Zizou wasn't there to help them. The last moments of his football career were also the worst moments of his career. Would he always be remembered for that one awful act?

Zinedine was devastated as he sat in the dressing room afterwards. He wanted to apologise to the other players but he didn't know what to say. There were no excuses for his bad behaviour. As captain, he should have led by example, just like he had in every other game. He still won the Golden Ball for the best player in the tournament but he had wanted to say goodbye with the World Cup trophy, not a red card.

It didn't change everything that Zinedine had done for France over the previous twelve years, however. As the President Jacques Chirac said to him, 'I know that you are sad and disappointed but what I want to tell you is that the whole country is extremely proud of you. You have honoured the country with your exceptional qualities and your fantastic fighting spirit.'

Zinedine couldn't believe that his career was over. The World Cup, the Euros, the Champions League, the Italian league, the Spanish league – he had won them all. 'Not bad for a boy from La Castellane!' he thought to himself.

With his quick feet, X-ray vision and incredible football brain, Zinedine had always had the talent. But thanks to his friends, family, teammates and coaches, he had developed the patience and teamwork to go on and achieve his dreams. Zizou, whose parents had come from Algeria, had retired as France's greatest hero.

CHAPTER 2

LA CASTELLANE

'Yazid, are you okay?' Malika called out as she ran into the bedroom where her four sons slept. She had been woken up by the screams of the youngest, Zinedine Yazid Zidane.

Malika knew exactly what was wrong – it was the third time it had happened that week. She stroked Yazid's head and wiped away his tears.

'Everything's fine,' she whispered, hoping that her three other sons, Nourredine, Farid and Madjid, would be able to get back to sleep. 'It was just a nightmare – you're safe here at home.'

'Where's Dad?' Yazid asked. 'There was a strange man by the door over there. I saw him!'

'No, there's no-one there. It was just a bad dream,' Malika replied. 'Your dad is at work. He's safe too, I promise. He has to work night shifts this week. He'll be back by the time you wake up in, the morning.'

But when he had nightmares, Yazid could never go back to sleep. Instead, he lay there in the darkness, listening to his brothers breathing and the late-night fighting and police sirens outside the window. There was always something going on in La Castellane. A lot of people in France thought that the estate in Marseille was a bad and dangerous place to live but, for Yazid, it was home. He had his family with him and he had his friends next door. You could always hear music and you could always play football. What more did you need?

Like many of their neighbours in La Castellane, Yazid's parents had come to France from Africa. Smaïl and Malika left Algeria when their country was in the middle of a civil war. Life was safer in France and there were more jobs available, especially as they already spoke French. Smaïl worked in a warehouse. It was a tough job, night shifts were difficult, but his wages paid for their food and their apartment. His family were all healthy and happy – that was the most important thing. But even when his sons were very young, Smaïl tried to prepare them for adult life.

'Life is never easy for people like us,' he told them one day at the dinner table. Yazid and his brothers always listened carefully. 'When you move to a new country, you have to work twice as hard as everyone else. Keep going and never give up!'

Once Yazid could see daylight creeping through the curtains, he knew that his dad would be home soon. Finally, Smaïl unlocked the front door, dropped his work bag in the hallway and opened his sons' bedroom door a little bit.

Sometimes, Yazid pretended to be sleeping when his dad came back but this time, he waved and smiled.

'Why are you awake?' his dad whispered.

'I had another nightmare,' Yazid replied.

'Well, I'm home now,' Smaïl said, ruffling his son's hair. He let out a big yawn. 'So get some sleep –

...oon as my head hits

...got up with his brothers and
...st for them in the kitchen, while
Sh...

'Shh...hhhhh!' she whispered, putting a finger
to her lips. 'Farid, if you want to make that much
noise, go outside!'

As soon as they had scoffed down enough cereal,
Nourredine, Farid and Madjid rushed out of the
door, down the many stairs of the tower block, and
out into the Place de la Tartane, La Castellane's
central square. They had just enough time for a
quick game of football before school. But Yazid
wasn't allowed to go with them – he was still
too young.

'As soon as you turn five, you can join them,' his
mum told him again and again.

Yazid tried to count down the days until his fifth
birthday: 365, 364, 363, 362, 361... 'Mum, how old
am I now?' he asked.

'Four years and...' Malika checked the calendar

and did the maths in her head. '...275 days. So only 90 more days to go, little man!'

As he waited for the big day, Yazid had work to do. He wanted to make sure that he was ready for his debut in the Place de la Tartane, so he practised his dribbling and shooting skills in the living room, while his mum washed up their breakfast plates. He used whatever he could find – a football, a tennis ball, even a rolled-up sock if he had to.

Malika didn't notice that Yazid wasn't with her in the kitchen until she heard the noise.

Smash!

She sighed loudly – not again! Her son was breaking things all the time and they didn't have the money to replace everything. Even when he hadn't slept all night, Yazid had far too much energy to be kept indoors all day. So what could they do? If Yazid's brothers kept a close eye on him, perhaps he could go out and play with them? No, she would never forgive herself if something bad happened to him.

Malika picked up the dustpan and brush, and went to check on the damage. Smaïl was awake now too, rubbing the sleep from his eyes. As he walked into the living room, he was ready to give his youngest son a big telling-off.

Yazid hadn't meant to kick the tennis ball so hard. It was an accident. In his head, he was about to score the winning goal in the cup final and he got carried away with his shot. As the lamp fell over, the lightbulb smashed. He knew that his parents would be really mad at him.

But when Smaïl saw Yazid standing there, looking very guilty with his hands behind his back, his anger suddenly disappeared. He could still remember being that young and lively. He took the dustpan and brush from his wife and cleared up the broken bulb. While Yazid wasn't looking, Malika took the tennis ball and hid it away in the cupboard.

'Son, I can't wait until you turn five!' his dad said.

'Me too!' his mum said.

'Me too!' Yazid said.

CHAPTER 3

THE PLACE DE LA TARTANE

'How are you feeling on your big day?' Smaïl asked his youngest son at the breakfast table.

'I feel great, thanks!' Yazid told his dad. Then he turned and shouted towards his bedroom. 'Madjid, Farid, Nourredine, are you ready yet?'

'No!' they replied. Farid was only just getting out of the shower.

'Well, hurry up!' Yazid called out. He had been waiting a long time for this moment.

It was Yazid's fifth birthday and so after his bowl of cereal, his parents put a candle in a small slice of cake and sang 'Happy Birthday' to him. His brothers thought they were too cool to join in with the singing but they clapped at the end. Malika had baked the cake herself and it was delicious.

It was a brilliant start to the day and it was about to get even better. Usually, Yazid was still in his pyjamas at breakfast. But today, he was fully dressed and wide awake, even though he had been too excited to sleep. It was time to make his football debut in the Place de la Tartane.

Smaïl and Malika smiled to each other as they watched their youngest son doing warm-up stretches in the hallway. 'Hopefully Yazid will come back exhausted!' his mum thought to herself.

Finally, all of his brothers were ready to go. Yazid raced down the stairs and along the path to the square. He practised his kick as he ran.

'Hey, slow down!' Nourredine shouted. 'Mum said that we have to look after you.'

When they arrived, a few kids were already kicking a ball around. The two goalposts were set up – jumpers at one end and rocks at the other. With handshakes and high-fives, Yazid was accepted into the football gang.

'Before you start playing, we need to talk you through the rules,' Madjid said. 'You're the youngest kid, so please don't be a crybaby! Otherwise, we won't let you play again, okay? If anyone fouls you, you have to get back up and keep running.'

'And if your teammates don't pass to you, you can't get upset,' Farid added. 'There are some really good players in La Castellane and you'll just have to wait your turn on the ball.'

Yazid nodded and nodded until his neck started to hurt. 'Okay, can we play football now?'

The match kicked off – the Zidane brothers versus four of their neighbours. Yazid ran and ran and fell over and fell over. But he never complained about the cuts and bruises.

'Are you okay?' Nourredine asked, helping him to his feet.

Yazid nodded and smiled. 'I've never felt better!'

Some of the older boys were really strong and there was nothing that he could do about that. One day, he would be that strong too but for now, Yazid focused on other skills – controlling the ball and passing. He tried to stay calm on the ball and keep things simple. As long as he didn't make any big mistakes, they would let him play again the next day.

Besides, Yazid didn't want to be a show-off like his brother Farid. Every time he got the ball, Farid tried to dribble past everyone but he usually gave the ball away.

'Pass it!' Madjid shouted at him angrily. He was in lots of space for an easy shot at goal.

'Shut up!' Farid shouted back. The Zidane brothers were always fighting on the football pitch. But as soon as the game was over, they went back to being good friends again.

Nourredine, as the oldest, was in charge of keeping an eye on the time. If they didn't check, they would just keep playing all day long. In the square, they had all the fun and freedom they could want.

'Right, we're going to be late for school if we don't leave now,' he told the others eventually.

'No, if we run, we can make it there in five minutes,' Farid argued. 'Let's play "Next Goal Wins"!'

The Zidane brothers were losing by two goals, so this was their only chance of victory. As Farid dribbled forward, three defenders ran in to tackle him. They knew how much he hated to pass the ball. But this was 'Next Goal Wins' and the Zidane brothers would do anything to win. Farid looked up and passed to his youngest brother.

'Yaz, I'm here!'

'Yaz, play the one-two!'

Yazid could hear his brothers calling for the ball but he didn't rush. He protected the ball and looked for the perfect pass to play into the perfect gap to win the game. There was no hurry, even if his brothers didn't agree.

'Come on, Yaz! What are you doing?'

'We haven't got all day!'

As Nourredine made a clever run behind the defenders, Yazid kicked the ball into his path. His friend Doudou stretched out his leg but he couldn't quite stop it. Nourredine took one touch and shot past the keeper.

'What a pass!' Farid cheered as he lifted his

youngest brother into the air. On his debut, Yazid was the hero.

'I can't wait to play again after school!' he told his brothers happily.

It was the first of many match-winning performances in the Place de la Tartane. There was no stopping him now. Every morning, Yazid kicked the ball against the wall until the other kids arrived, and every evening he played in the square until the other kids went home.

Malika was happy for her children to play football in the square until dinner time. It tired them out, kept them safe and out of trouble, and she could keep an eye on them from the kitchen. If she needed them, all she had to do was open the window and shout down 'Food!' and usually they'd come running.

As he got older, Yazid became more confident at dribbling and shooting but he stayed very modest. When the other kids were practising new tricks, he always joined in but once he had perfected them, he saved them for very special occasions.

'You're the best player here,' Doudou told him one

day. 'So why don't you show off more, Yaz?'

He shrugged. 'What's the point, unless it helps us to win?'

It was Yazid's quick feet and killer pass that helped his team to win. While others sprinted around the pitch as fast as they could, Yazid took his time, especially when he had the ball. While others panted, he glided.

He did have one trademark trick of his own, however, that he called the 'Marseille Roulette'. As a defender approached, he dragged the ball back with one foot and then used the other foot to spin away into space. It worked every time.

Yazid saw the game differently to the others. He had a special talent and it was time to put it to the test outside of the Place de la Tartane.

CHAPTER 4

TOURNAMENT FOOTBALL

'Yaz, have you heard what the prize is today?' his friend Malek Kourane asked excitedly.

They were playing together for their local team AS Foresta in a summer tournament. Until then, Yazid hadn't even thought about a prize. The trophy and a winner's medal was all he wanted.

'If we win, we all get brand-new bikes!' Malek continued.

Yazid's face lit up. Other than new football boots, a bike was what every nine-year-old kid wanted. Their friends at La Castellane would be so jealous.

'Come on, guys!' Yazid shouted to his teammates

as the first match kicked off. 'We've got to play really well today!'

Yazid was AS Foresta's captain and chief playmaker. From the centre of midfield, he created the chances for Malek to score the goals. Their partnership was one of the best in the whole of Marseille.

Yazid used his strength and quick feet to protect the ball. He knew the exact run that Malek would make and so he waited for the perfect moment. When he saw the striker move, he hit a beautiful diagonal pass to him. As Malek entered the box, a defender tripped him. Penalty!

Yazid pumped his fist but his smile quickly disappeared as Malek collected the ball and got ready to take the spot-kick.

'Hey, that's my job!' Yazid shouted as he rushed over to the penalty area. He tried to grab the ball but Malek wouldn't let go.

'Let me take this – I won the penalty!' Malek argued.

'But I'm the penalty taker.'

'But I'm the goalscorer.'

Yazid wasn't happy but he knew that Malek wouldn't give up. 'Okay but if you miss, you're in big trouble!' he said.

Malek stepped up and kicked the ball towards the bottom corner. But the goalkeeper dived the right way and saved it! As he stood with his hands on his head, Malek looked at Yazid. His teammate didn't say a word but he didn't need to. His anger was obvious.

Yazid kept creating chances but Malek had completely lost his confidence in front of goal. His shots went wide, over the bar, straight at the keeper – anywhere but in the back of the net. Somehow, AS Foresta lost the match and were knocked out of the tournament.

Yazid managed to keep himself calm until they were walking home to La Castellane.

'You owe me a new bike,' he muttered under his breath.

'What?' Malek asked.

'YOU OWE ME A NEW BIKE!!!' Yazid shouted, giving him a strong shove.

They were soon friends again, but Malek didn't

take another penalty for AS Foresta. He didn't dare.

When he was ten, Yazid joined another local team, US Saint-Henri. He was playing at a higher level now but that didn't scare him. He quickly became the star again.

'Well played, Yaz!' the US Saint-Henri coach said at the final whistle. Yazid had scored the winner in their first game of the summer tournament.

Smaïl was there at the football ground, proudly watching his youngest son. 'What a strike!' he clapped.

Yazid smiled but he looked pale and a little unsteady on his feet.

'Are you feeling alright?' his dad asked.

'It's so hot!' he replied. 'And I didn't sleep very well last night.'

'Another nightmare?'

Yazid nodded bashfully. He was too old to be having bad dreams but sometimes he couldn't help it.

'Take it easy in this next game,' his dad said. 'You've got a whole day of football ahead of you!'

Yazid started slowly but US Saint-Henri needed him

at his best. They were heading for a draw with only a few minutes to go. His teammates were rushing around trying to score but that wasn't Yazid's style. He looked for a good pass to play but when there weren't many options, he decided to be inventive.

'Time for the Marseille Roulette!' Yazid said to himself.

He dribbled one way, then quickly dragged the ball back and spun the other way. It was a magical bit of skill that totally fooled the defender. Yazid had created an extra bit of space and his shot flew into the top corner.

Goooooooooooooooooooooooaaaaaaaaaaaaaaaaaaallllll llllllllllllllllllll!!!!!!!!!!!!!!!

He had scored the winner again!

As soon as the match finished, Smaïl told his son to sit down and gave him a bottle of water and a chocolate bar to boost his energy levels. He looked even paler than before and he could hardly keep his eyes open.

'How are you feeling now?' his dad asked after Yazid had rested a few minutes.

Yazid nodded but he was too tired to speak. As the next match was about to start, he tried to get up but his legs felt really weak and wobbly.

'That's it – we're going home!' his dad said.

'No, we can't!'

'You can't keep playing in that state.'

Smaïl went to speak to the US Saint-Henri manager. 'I'm afraid I have to take Yazid home. He's not feeling well.'

The coach shook his head. 'You can't do that.'

Smaïl looked confused. 'Why can't I do that?'

'Because we'll lose without him!'

He looked over at his son, who was sat with his head between his knees as if he might be sick. There was no way that he could carry on playing. 'Sorry, I'm taking him home,' Smaïl said.

Without Yazid, US Saint-Henri were knocked out of the tournament. If they didn't want to look after their star player properly, Yazid would just have to find another club that would.

CHAPTER 5

FRANCE VS ALGERIA

Football coaches loved Yazid's unique football style.
With the ball at his feet, he was clever, elegant, skilful
and calm. But every now and again, he became the
opposite. Sometimes, if someone was rude to him, he
got really angry and stormed off the pitch, or started
arguing with opponents.

'What on earth happened to you today?' Smaïl
asked his son when they got home. The referee had
dragged Yazid off the pitch to stop him fighting.

Yazid sat on the sofa in silence with his arms folded
across his chest and a big frown on his face. But
eventually, once he had calmed down, he tried to
explain.

'Their midfielder kept calling me horrible names,' he mumbled towards the floor.

'That's no excuse!' his dad replied sternly. 'What have I always told you? You have to be strong and ignore the insults. And you can't just turn to violence every time you're upset.'

Yazid nodded slowly but he hadn't told his dad everything. 'H-he said that I wasn't really French because my dad was from Africa.'

Smaïl needed time to think, to find the right words to help his son. 'Yaz, where were you born?' he asked finally.

'Marseille.'

'And where is Marseille?'

'In France.'

'And where have you lived for your whole life so far?'

'In Marseille, in France.'

'Exactly,' his dad said. 'Yaz, you *are* French. But you also have an African heritage and it's important to remember where your family came from. So next time someone mentions Africa, stay calm and be proud!'

During the 1982 World Cup in Spain, the Zidanes

had two favourite teams to cheer for – France *and* Algeria.

'I don't think Algeria will last long here but it's just great to see them in the tournament,' Smaïl said as they all sat down to watch Algeria's first match against West Germany on TV.

'Dad, don't be so negative!' Nourredine complained and his brothers agreed. They had high hopes for 'The Desert Foxes' and one player in particular – Number 14, Djamel Zidane. Yazid lied and told all his friends that he was his uncle.

When Algeria took the lead, there were loud cheers all around La Castellane.

'We told you!' Yazid shouted joyfully to his dad.

Smaïl smiled but the match wasn't over yet. When West Germany equalised, they feared the worst.

But a minute later, Salah Assad made a brilliant run down the left wing. His cross flew past the West Germany defenders and there was Lakhdar Belloumi at the back post for a tap-in. 2-1!

'Yessssssssssssssssssssssssssssssssssssssss!' the Zidane brothers shouted and this time their dad joined in

the celebrations. It was a moment that the people of
Algeria would never forget. When the final whistle
blew, they ran out into the estate and jumped around
as if they had won the World Cup.

'When I'm older, I'm going to play for Algeria!'
Yazid told his brothers excitedly.

'Why would you want to do that?' Farid asked.
'You could play for France and they're much better.'

Yazid soon saw that his brother was right. After
beating West Germany, Algeria lost 2-0 to Austria. It
was a disappointing defeat and it meant that Algeria
were knocked out of the tournament, even after a 3-2
win over Chile.

'It's not fair!' Yazid complained, but his dad just
shrugged and moved on to supporting France instead.

Yazid was soon supporting France too. They had
a great team, and especially in midfield, which was
his favourite position. Alain Giresse, Michel Platini
and Jean Tigana were three of the best players in
the world.

'Tigana was born in Africa, just like me,' Smaïl
told his sons proudly. 'He came to France from Mali.

Maybe there's still hope for my football career!'

Yazid and his brothers laughed and laughed. The idea of their dad playing professional football was very funny.

In the semi-finals, France were up against West Germany. 'If Algeria can beat them then surely France can too!' Yazid thought to himself. But the match wasn't that simple or that boring. Instead, it was like a roller coaster, full of exciting ups and downs. Germany scored first but Platini equalised.

'Come on!' Yazid shouted, pumping his fists at the TV screen.

After sixty minutes, Platini played an incredible long pass to defender Patrick Battiston. He was through on goal.

'Yes, he's going to score!' Yazid screamed, jumping up out of his chair.

As Battiston shot wide, the German goalkeeper Harald Schumacher charged into him at full speed.

'How is that not a foul?' Yazid complained. 'Look, he can't even get up.'

But the referee waved 'play on' and Battiston had

to be taken off the field on a stretcher. The amazing match continued. In extra time, France took a 3-1 lead but West Germany fought back to 3-3.

'Penalties!' his brothers cheered together. They loved the drama of spot-kicks but when it was his own country playing, Yazid had to peek out from behind a cushion.

After ten penalties, the score was 4-4. In sudden death, Schumacher saved the French penalty.

'That guy shouldn't even be on the pitch!' Smaïl shouted angrily at the screen.

West Germany scored to make it through to the World Cup final. Yazid wiped the tears from his face and he wasn't the only one.

'Why didn't Tigana take one?' Yazid asked his dad later that evening.

Smaïl shrugged. 'Perhaps he was too nervous,' he suggested. 'I don't think I could take one. There's so much pressure on you!'

'I could take a penalty and I would score,' Yazid said confidently. 'When I'm older, I'm going to play for France and we're going to win the World Cup!'

CHAPTER 6

SEPTÈMES

'Yazid is one of the best young midfielders I've ever seen,' Robert Centenaro told Smaïl. The coach had been keeping a close eye on the eleven-year-old for months but now it was time for action. That's why he was talking to the boy's dad. 'I'm desperate for him to come and play for Septèmes. We'll do our very best to help him become an even better player.'

Smaïl liked the coach's enthusiasm but there was one big problem. 'La Castellane is a long way from Septèmes-les-Vallons,' he said. 'How will Yazid get to the practices and matches?'

Robert already had an answer for that. 'Don't worry, I've got a car and I already collect kids from all over Marseille. One more won't make a difference!'

Yazid was stood next to his dad and as he listened, he grew more and more excited. Playing for Septèmes would be a great new challenge at exactly the right time. After US Saint-Henri, he was ready for the next level.

'Have you ever been to La Castellane?' Smaïl asked. He wanted to make sure that Robert knew what he was agreeing to. The estate could be a dangerous place, especially for people who didn't live there.

'No, but I've heard about it,' Robert answered with a confident smile. 'I'll be fine. See you at 5pm on Wednesday?'

Smaïl nodded and shook the coach's hand. He was sure that his son would be well looked after at Septèmes. 'Are you looking forward to it, Yaz?'

'I can't wait!' he replied.

At 5pm on Wednesday, Robert was there, just as he had promised, ringing their apartment buzzer. But at 6pm, they were still there in La Castellane. They tried to drive away but the tiny car wouldn't move. Robert got out to check what was wrong and found four flat tyres. The Septèmes coach wasn't happy but he didn't give up on Yazid.

'I'll just stay in my car next time!' Robert joked to Smaïl.

When Yazid finally got to training, he quickly showed off his stylish passing. In the big final match, he was at the centre of everything. No-one could get the ball off him because of his strength and quick feet. Yazid moved the ball from side to side until he found the killer through-ball, or the space to dribble forward and shoot. He made football look so easy and classy.

'What did I tell you?' Robert said to one of the other Septèmes coaches on the sidelines. They both had big grins on their faces. 'That kid's going to be a star!'

Yazid went straight into the Septèmes starting line-up and he was soon their best player. Even when their opponents put lots of pressure on him in midfield, he still found clever ways out.

'How does it feel to have a superpower?' his new

teammate Julien laughed. 'You've got X-ray football vision – you see things that no-one else can see!'

Yazid was really enjoying his time at Septèmes, especially the away games. He had never left Marseille before, but suddenly he was travelling to other parts of Southern France like Montpellier and Perpignan to play football. They never had time to explore these places but he saw some impressive views from the windows of the team coach.

'Wow, look! There's still snow on the top of the mountains,' Julien pointed.

Yazid couldn't believe it. His teachers had shown him photos of the Alps before but now the peaks were right there, looming up in front of him. It was the most amazing sight he had ever seen. Yazid felt a very long way away from La Castellane.

'So where were you this weekend?' Doudou liked to tease him on Monday mornings back at school. 'London? Barcelona? New York?'

Yazid laughed. 'No, we had a home game!'

But nothing could stop Doudou's comedy act. 'I'm sorry that sometimes you have to spend a few hours with us little people of La Castellane. It must be so dull for you now!'

'Shut up!' Yazid said, giving his friend a playful shove. 'You know I love it here – this is my home.'

'Not for long! Soon, you'll move to a big house in the middle of Marseille, or Paris. And then you'll forget all about us!'

Doudou's jokes only got worse when Yazid was invited to play a match for the French national youth team. Every time Yazid entered the classroom, Doudou bowed and pretended to kiss Yazid's feet.

'Can I help you with anything, sir?' Doudou asked in a funny voice.

'Yes, actually you can,' Yazid replied with a cheeky grin. 'Come and play football in the Place de la Tartane after school. I've got some new tricks to teach you little people of La Castellane!'

CHAPTER 7

EURO 84: BEST BIRTHDAY EVER

'Is the birthday boy awake yet?' Malika called out, as she opened the bedroom door slightly.

'Yes!' Yazid replied loudly, forgetting that his brothers were still sleeping. He had been awake for hours because his twelfth birthday was shaping up to be the best one yet.

First, there would be a family breakfast with lots of food and presents. Then he would head out into the Place de la Tartane for a big, long game of football with his friends. And, in the evening, he would watch the big match on TV: France vs Portugal in the semi-finals of Euro 1984.

'Are you hungry?' his mum asked.

'Yes!' Yazid replied.

By the time his brothers joined him at the table, Yazid was on his second bowl of cereal. For one day only, his parents couldn't tell him to slow down.

'Are you ready for your presents now?' his dad asked.

'Yes!' Yazid replied.

He unwrapped his first two gifts in a flash – a Marseille Football Club hat from his brothers, and a new book in his favourite series from his mum.

'Thanks, guys!' Yazid said.

Then he turned to his third and final present. He had left it until last on purpose because it was the most mysterious. It looked and felt like a cardboard box. As Yazid lifted it up, the box felt quite heavy and he could hear things moving inside.

'Just open it!' Smaïl cheered. He wasn't normally so impatient about presents. 'He must have bought me the best gift ever,' Yazid thought to himself. He was so excited.

As he tore off the wrapping paper, his eyes lit up. Written on the lid of the box were four letters that together spelled out a magical word – 'Kopa'. Could this present really be what he hoped it was? It could! Yazid opened the box to find a brand-new pair of Kopa football boots. They were the coolest boots around and they cost a lot of money.

'Wow, these are amazing!' he shouted, running over to hug his parents. 'Thank you, thank you, thank you!'

Seconds later, the boots were on his feet. They looked brilliant and they felt so light and springy – perfect for playing football. Suddenly, Yazid wasn't interested in his big breakfast anymore.

'Who wants to come with me to test them out?' he asked.

Smaïl stopped him straight away. 'Son, you can't wear those out in the square – you'll ruin them on the concrete. Wait until you play on grass tomorrow. Please promise me you'll look after those boots – we can't afford to buy you another pair!'

Yazid nodded and carefully took the boots off. 'I promise, Dad! I'll clean them every week. Football, anyone?'

His brothers didn't play much football in La Castellane anymore but that day was a special day. They all got dressed quickly and headed outside for a kick about.

The sun was shining brightly in a clear blue sky. Yazid had lots of reasons to smile. All of his friends were there in the Place de la Tartane waiting for him and they let him pick the teams on his birthday.

The match went on for hours. Yazid pretended he was France's Number 10 – Michel Platini. He ran from end to end, playing one-twos, through balls and clever flicks. With his socks rolled down like his hero, he even scored a brilliant chip over Doudou's head. Could his birthday get any better?

'Yaz, dinner's ready!' Malika shouted eventually.

It seemed too early to eat but then Yazid remembered – they needed to be finished in time to watch football on TV. 'Coming!' he called back.

France were the hosts of Euro 84 and so there was a great buzz of excitement around the country. Their semi-final against Portugal was taking place in Marseille at the Stade Vélodrome, just a few miles away from La Castellane. Yazid went to the window to listen for the noise of the crowd but he couldn't quite hear it. Not until France took the lead, anyway.

'*Allez les Bleus*!' the Zidane family shouted together.

France had added Luis Fernández to their midfield trio of Platini, Giresse and Tigana. They were now called the 'Magic Square' and Yazid loved watching their passing and movement. They were always in space to receive the ball and once they had it, they hardly ever lost it. France had lots of chances to score a second goal but the goalkeeper made some great saves.

Portugal didn't give up and with one minute to go in extra time, the score was 2-2. The match looked like it was heading to penalties again, just like their World Cup match against West Germany two years earlier.

'We can't lose two semi-finals in a row on penalties!' Yazid said. He already had his cushion ready to hide behind.

Fernández passed forward to Tigana, who dribbled into the penalty area.

'Yes, come on!' Yazid cheered at the screen.

The angle was too wide for Tigana to shoot and so he pulled it back for Platini. The defenders dived at his feet to block the shot, but Platini shot high into the top of the net.

Gooooooooooooooooooooaaaaaaaaaaaaaaaaaaaalllll llllllllllllllllllllll!!!!!!!!!!!!!!!

Yazid ran around the apartment, cheering wildly. What a birthday! First, a new pair of football boots – and now France were through to the Euro 84 final. On TV, the players celebrated together and in La Castellane, the neighbours did the same.

'Now we just have to beat Spain!' Yazid said to his brothers.

The final was in Paris at the Parc des Princes but there was a great atmosphere everywhere in France. The nation had never won a World Cup or European Championship before.

'This is our big chance!' people kept saying.

In the end, the final wasn't as exciting as the semi-final. Platini scored a free-kick and, in the last minute, Bruno Bellone made it 2-0. As soon as the match was over, Yazid went outside to join the big party in La Castellane.

Campeones, Campeones, Olé Olé Olé!

'One day, I'm going to play for France,' Yazid told his brothers again, 'and I'm going to help us win our first World Cup!'

CHAPTER 8

SCOUTED

Jean Varraud knew the south of France very well. As a youth coach for AS Cannes, a team in the French second division, one of his favourite things was discovering young local talent. Montpellier, Nice, Toulouse – every weekend, Jean got in his car and travelled to watch highly-rated young players. Ninety-nine per cent of the time, nothing very special caught his eye and he went home a little disappointed. But the long journeys were all worth it for that magical one per cent.

Septèmes-les-Vallons was a two-hour drive from Cannes and Jean knew the route well. Usually he travelled an extra twenty minutes to go to Marseille but that particular day, he stopped in Septèmes. Their Under-15s team was on a long winning streak and Jean had been hearing very good things about their attacking midfielder, Zinedine Yazid Zidane.

'Well, let's see what you've got, kid,' Jean said to himself as he got out of his car and stretched his legs.

It didn't take the AS Cannes youth coach long to work out which kid on the pitch was the superstar. There was nothing very special about the boy's appearance – black hair, average height, neither really skinny nor really muscly. No, what was special was his feet and what they could do with the ball.

'Wow!' Jean said out loud as the boy dragged the ball away from a defender, spun and played a brilliant pass out to the wing. 'How did he do that?'

The other Septèmes players weren't brilliant individuals but their leader helped them to form a great team. The kid went past one player, then another and then another. He wasn't showing off; he was always looking for his teammates. He passed left, he passed right; when there were no options ahead of him, he was happy to play a backward pass; and when he spotted a great run, he played the perfect forward pass. Jean knew that he was watching a great football brain at work.

'He plays more like a thirty-four-year-old than a fourteen-year-old!' Jean laughed to himself. He had that great feeling that he got when he found that magical one per cent. 'We need to sign him before another club does!'

Jean had never seen a playmaker like Yazid. Often, skilful players could be lazy and greedy but this kid was working really hard for his team. He played with determination and he seemed to enjoy the physical battle in midfield. Thanks to his dad and his days in La Castellane, Yazid had learned never to give up.

'A warrior with the feet of an artist' – that was how Jean Varraud eagerly described Yazid to Jean Fernandez, the AS Cannes first team manager.

Fernandez couldn't help laughing. It sounded like a winning combination but could this kid really be that good? 'Okay, fine, I'll come and watch him in training later today!'

Yazid was enjoying his trial at Cannes. Everyone at

Septèmes was sad to see him go but they understood that this was a great chance for him to join a professional club. It was an important time in his football career, where he needed to keep challenging himself.

He could always hear his dad's voice in his head, saying, 'You have to work twice as hard as everyone else.'

That's exactly what Yazid was doing. He was playing with better players and that was helping him to become even better too. The defenders didn't give him time on the ball to think. Instead, he had to protect the ball really well and make quicker decisions. Dribble? Shoot? Pass? He chose a lovely long pass from right to left.

'Excellent, Yaz!' Jean Varraud shouted, clapping loudly.

Once first team training was over, Fernandez joined Varraud on the sidelines. Luckily, Yazid didn't notice Fernandez watching him and so he didn't think there was anything to be nervous about. He played his natural game, using his quick feet to keep the ball until one of his teammates was in space for the pass.

Fernandez didn't say anything until the practice was over. Varraud thought that the first team manager wasn't that impressed with Yazid but he was wrong.

'Jean, you deserve a very big bonus!' Fernandez said with a smile.

'What do you mean?' Varraud asked.

'That kid is a genius! Why on earth is he not playing for PSG or Marseille?'

Varraud shrugged. 'He can be a bit too aggressive sometimes but we can definitely work on that. I'm glad that you agree with me.'

'That kid could be the future of this club,' Fernandez said. 'I'll let you train him well for a couple of years and then he'll be joining my first team squad!'

AS Cannes were desperate to sign Yazid but there was still one problem to solve.

'He can't travel from La Castellane every day,' Smaïl told Varraud. 'It's just too far and too tiring.'

Jean nodded. 'I agree. We want Yazid to join our academy here in Cannes. We want him to feel settled here. It's the best place for developing his skills.'

'But where will he live?' Malika asked. Yazid looked so excited next to her but he wasn't thinking about anything except football. She would never stop her son from following his dream but she wanted to make sure that he would be safe and happy.

'Don't worry – we'll find a family for Yazid to live with,' Jean reassured her. 'We want his life to be as normal as possible.'

Malika smiled but she couldn't help worrying. This was a great opportunity for Yazid but how would he cope at a new club in a new city?

'At least we'll only be two hours away,' she said to Smaïl as they drove home. On the back seat, Yazid relaxed with a big smile on his face. He was an AS Cannes player now.

CHAPTER 9

CALMING DOWN AT CANNES

'Hello, the Zidane family?' Malika answered the phone.

A few seconds later, she mouthed three words to her husband – 'It's Yazid again.' There was a sad, worried look on her face.

At first, life in Cannes was very difficult for Yazid. After a few weeks of living in a dormitory at the academy with the other young players, he moved into the house of Jean-Claude Elineau, the club's Director of Football. It was a better environment for him and the Elineau family were really kind and supportive, but it still wasn't the same as being back in La Castellane with his own family.

There were no big, loud meals and there was no Place de la Tartane for when he just wanted to step outside and play some fun street football. Yazid was desperate to become a professional footballer but he wanted to be happy too. What if Cannes never felt like home?

'Have you made any friends on your team?' Malika asked.

Yazid sniffed and wiped the tears from his face. He always called from a phone box at the end of the street. He didn't want the family he was living with to know that he was so upset all the time.

'They're all nice guys and a few of them are from Marseille,' he replied eventually. 'But I miss you!'

Malika hated to think of her son all alone and far from home. But if she let him give up now, he might regret it in a few months. 'I miss you too!' she said. 'We can't wait to come and visit you in two weeks. If you're still not enjoying it by then, we'll bring you home. How does that sound?'

'Okay,' Yazid replied.

The problem was that even the football wasn't

going that well. Most of his teammates had been playing at Cannes for years and so he had a lot of catching up to do.

In one of his first matches, Yazid ran into the penalty area as the winger swung in a great cross. It was the perfect height for a header but Yazid ducked.

'What are you doing?' one of his teammates shouted at him angrily.

Jean Varraud was quick to protect his new player. 'Hey, I don't want to hear any negativity out there! If you don't have kind, encouraging words to say to your teammates, you should say nothing at all.'

But he also made a mental note: 'teach Yazid how to head the ball'.

Jean had a long list of things to work on. Most importantly, he needed to help Yazid to stay calm on the pitch. He was very competitive and if an opponent said something rude to him, he just exploded.

'I know it's not nice when someone calls you a horrible name but you can't react like that. Why do you think other players do it to you?' Jean asked.

Yazid had been taken off to cool down. He stared at the ground and shrugged.

'It's because they know that you're better than them and it's the only way they can stop you,' Jean explained. 'When you get angry, they win. If you just ignore them, *you* win.'

The AS Cannes youth coach knew that Yazid was worth the extra attention. You could teach a kid discipline, but there was no way that you could teach a kid Yazid's level of technique. That was outstanding, natural talent.

Not everyone, however, loved the boy's playing style. Other coaches at AS Cannes thought Yazid needed to adapt his game:

'He's too slow – it's always pass, pass, pass. It's goals that win matches!'

'Does he even know what football's about? He seems more interested in playing nice little touches than trying to score!'

But Jean disagreed. Yes, Yazid did prefer to play elegant, flowing football but what was wrong with that? He was also determined to win. You only had to look at the focus and fire in his eyes, once the match kicked off, to know that.

'I refuse to build a boring football robot!' Jean Varraud complained to Fernandez. 'He's got real, creative flair and this club needs that.'

Fernandez just laughed. 'You don't need to tell me! Keep doing what you're doing and Yazid is going to be the real deal. Who knows, he might even be the captain of France one day!'

When the Zidane family came to visit, they were pleased to find a happier boy.

'Jean says that they might start letting me train with the first team next season,' he said, with his voice full of excitement. 'Then when I turn sixteen, hopefully I can start playing in proper matches!'

Malika laughed. 'It's so nice to hear you sounding so cheerful. I feared you might come crying into my arms like you used to when you were five years old!'

'Mum, stop embarrassing me!' Yazid shouted but he was smiling about it.

He wasn't yet ready to tell his family about the other reason for his happiness.

CHAPTER 10

ZINEDINE AND VÉRONIQUE

His Cannes teammates were always trying to get him to go out with them at the weekends after matches.

'Come on, it'll be fun!' Guillaume told him. 'We'll go to a café and I promise we won't get home late. You need to relax and maybe we'll meet some nice girls!'

The first few times, he said no. He was a shy person and sitting in a room full of noise wasn't really his idea of fun or relaxation. But eventually, he agreed to go. He knew that it was important to do things as a team and he didn't want the others to think that he was really boring.

As he sat there, half-listening to his teammates'

loud jokes, he looked around the café. There were a few other big groups of people chatting but then, in the corner, he saw a very pretty, dark-haired young woman on her own. She was reading a book and writing things down in a notebook. He watched her get up and order another coffee from the bar.

'Are you okay?' Guillaume called out from the other end of their table. 'Feel free to say something at some point – we won't bite!'

He laughed along and then stood up. 'Who wants another Coca-Cola?'

He felt confident at first but, once he got to the bar, he panicked. What could he say to her? What did people usually talk about?

'Are you a student?' he asked, finally.

The young woman smiled and nodded. 'Yes, I'm studying dance at a youth arts academy. Are you a student too?'

He had only thought about asking questions, not answering them too! 'Yes, er, um, no. I mean, I'm a footballer. Well, I'm training to become a footballer.'

The woman laughed and that helped him to

feel a little bit more relaxed. As they chatted, they discovered that they were both new to Cannes. They quickly bonded over the pain of moving away from home and missing their families.

'Sorry, I better go back to my teammates,' he said after a while. Out of the corner of his eye, he could see them all looking at him and signalling that they wanted their drinks. 'It was really nice to meet you. Sorry, I didn't even ask your name!'

The young woman laughed again. 'I'm Véronique,' she said.

'And I'm Zinedine,' he replied. After years of being called Yazid, he was now using his first name.

As he returned to the table, his teammates started clapping. 'Nice work!' Guillaume shouted.

Zinedine went bright red and hoped that Véronique wasn't watching.

Over the next few weeks he went back to the café several times and if Véronique was there, they sat and had coffee together. They talked about growing up in France in families that weren't French. He told her about his parents' journey from Algeria and she told

63

him about her family's journey from Spain.

'I'm a footballer and you're a dancer, but I think we've got a lot in common!' Zinedine said.

'I still don't believe that you're a footballer,' Véronique replied with a smile. 'Footballers are meant to be really arrogant and they don't talk about anything except football.'

He chuckled. 'That sounds like a lot of my teammates!'

Zinedine really liked spending time with Véronique. She was funny and kind, and when they were together he didn't even think about life back in La Castellane.

After training one day, he walked home with Guillaume. 'So how's your girlfriend?' his teammate asked with a wink.

'She's not my girlfriend!' Zinedine replied.

'Why not? Haven't you asked her out yet?'

'No, I think we're just friends. We only ever meet at that café.'

Guillaume rolled his eyes. 'You're a good guy, Yaz, but sometimes you're clueless! Next time you see her, you need to ask her out on a proper date. And I don't mean to that café!'

Zinedine nodded; his teammate was right. He needed to tell Véronique how he felt before she gave up on him.

He was really nervous as he spotted her sitting by the window at their usual table. The butterflies in his stomach were worse than when he played in a cup final. Should he ask her out straight away, or wait until they said goodbye?

'Are you okay?' she asked as they hugged. 'You look pale and you're sweating.'

'I, err, ran here,' Zinedine lied. 'My coach wants me to build up my stamina.'

He ordered a coffee and sat down opposite Véronique. She started telling him a story about a dance rehearsal but she could see that he wasn't really listening to her.

'Are you sure you're okay?' she asked.

Zinedine knew it was time to be brave. 'W-would you like to go on a date with me?'

Véronique's laughter confused him. What was so

funny? Had he made a stupid mistake? Then she saw his disappointed face.

'Sorry, of course I'll go on a date with you,' she said, smiling. 'I was laughing because my friends told me that if you didn't ask me out today, then I should ask *you*!'

Phew! Zinedine felt very relieved and happy. 'I've heard there's a nice Spanish restaurant by the waterfront. Wait, you do like Spanish food, right?'

'Of course, that sounds great.'

Soon, Zinedine and Véronique were calling each other every night and meeting up every weekend.

'You never really tell me about your football,' she said as they shared a dessert. 'Are you a really good player?'

Zinedine shrugged modestly. 'I'm not too bad, I guess.'

CHAPTER 11

THE START OF
GREAT THINGS

'You really think he's ready?' Jean Fernandez asked
Jean Varraud. 'He's still only sixteen!'

The youth coach nodded positively. 'I promise! If
you pick him, you won't regret it.'

Zinedine had been training with the AS Cannes
first team for months and he was improving rapidly.
He was now six feet tall and he had added more
power to his winning combination of determination
and skill. Cannes had won promotion to the French
first division, Ligue 1, but there was always room for
a new young superstar.

'Well, I'll blame you if it all goes wrong!' Jean
Fernandez warned with a smile. He knew how

important first team experience was for young players but he didn't want to rush things with Zinedine. What if he got injured or lost his cool and got sent off? That could really knock the boy's confidence.

As the 1988–89 season came to an end, AS Cannes were sitting comfortably in mid-table. The regular players were tired, so fresh legs were needed. Jean Fernandez decided that it was time for Zinedine to make his debut.

'Sorry, you won't be playing for us this weekend,' Jean Varraud told the youngster after a midweek training session, 'because you're playing for the first team away at Nantes!'

It was the best news that Zinedine had ever received. His seventeenth birthday was still a month away but his big wish was coming true early! It was one thing practising with his heroes like Guy Mengual and Zlatko Vujovi but now he would be playing in the same team as them in front of thousands of supporters.

Jean Varraud saw the fear spread across Zinedine's face. 'Don't worry, you'll be great!' the coach told him, giving him a big pat on the back.

Thursday and Friday passed so slowly. Even though he was very nervous, Zinedine couldn't wait for Saturday to arrive. He had been dreaming of the day when he would put on the white and red AS Cannes shirt for the first time and run out on to the field.

Zinedine was named as a substitute by Jean Fernandez, but he hoped to play at least a few minutes at the end. As he watched from the bench, his arms and legs were twitching. The score was 1-1 and Zinedine wanted to be out there on the pitch helping his team to win.

'Start warming up!' Fernandez shouted to him eventually.

Zinedine leapt to his feet and jogged up and down the touchline. He tried to take lots of long, deep breaths to calm his heartbeat down. He was about to make his debut! But if he was too excited, he wouldn't be able to play his usual elegant passes.

With fifteen minutes left, Zinedine entered the game. 'Don't panic, just keep it simple,' Fernandez told him. 'And enjoy it!'

After a few touches of the ball, Zinedine felt much better. He had worked hard to get into the first team. He deserved to be there and he wanted to prove it. He couldn't help Cannes to score a winning goal but he gave the fans and coaches a nice taster of what he could do – short passes, long passes, chips, flicks, tackles, shots.

'I didn't spot a single mistake!' Fernandez joked at the final whistle, giving him a big hug. 'Great job!'

Zinedine was delighted and his smile grew even wider when he was given a playing bonus.

'Wow, they're *paying* me to play football!' he kept saying to himself. It was still hard to believe.

Zinedine gave the money to his parents. 'In a few years, I'm going to buy you a lovely house in a quiet neighbourhood,' he told them. 'Then you can relax!'

In the 1989–90 season, Jean Fernandez played Zinedine in more matches. The youngster was impressing in every area except one: goals.

'I want to play him just behind the striker but we can only do that if he starts scoring,' the coach told the club president. 'Any ideas?'

A few days later, the president came up with a plan. 'Tell him that when he scores, we'll buy him a car!'

Fernandez told Zinedine the big news but by the end of the season, he still hadn't scored. It was becoming a problem and he was worried. What if Cannes gave up on him?

'The goals will come,' Jean Varraud told Zinedine when he came to ask for advice. 'You're thinking too much about it. Remember, you're still only eighteen!'

In February 1991, Nantes came to play against Cannes at the Stade Pierre de Coubertin. In the second half, Cannes were losing 1-0. Zinedine knew that it was now or never – he absolutely had to get that first goal.

As he made a great run between the central defenders, his teammate played the pass. It was a little bit behind Zinedine but he flicked the ball cleverly towards goal. The Cannes fans were up on their feet – could this be the moment that they had been waiting for?

Now the pressure was on. Zinedine had a defender chasing just behind him and a goalkeeper running towards him. In his head, he went back to the street games in the Place de la Tartane – what would the young Yazid have done in this difficult situation? Zinedine stayed calm and lifted the ball just over the keeper's outstretched arms from outside the area.

Goooooooooooooaaaaaaaaaaaaaallllllllllllllllllllllll!!!!!!!!!

Zinedine was so excited and relieved that he did a little dance. It was the start of great things.

'What a strike!' his teammates shouted as they ran over to hug him.

It was a moment that Zinedine would never forget. Cannes won 2-1 and the whole team celebrated wildly in the dressing room afterwards. Zinedine hadn't forgotten about his reward.

'So where's my car?' he asked the new manager, Boro Primorac.

Zinedine was expecting an old car but at a big party, the club president gave him a brand new red Renault Clio.

'We got it in the team colours, of course!' he joked.

Zinedine was amazed. He was a top professional footballer now and he had the car to prove it.

CHAPTER 12

ZIZOU AT BORDEAUX

After that brilliant first goal, Zinedine felt more comfortable about shooting. But scoring wasn't his main skill. He was Cannes' creative playmaker, setting up goals for strikers Carmelo Micciche and Amara Simba. In the 1990–91 season, the club finished fourth in Ligue 1.

'We'll be playing in the UEFA Cup next year!' Zinedine shouted as the whole team celebrated together. At the age of just eighteen, he had played in almost every game.

It was Cannes' best ever French league position but the great times didn't last long. Carmelo was sold to Nancy, while Amara went back to PSG. Suddenly, the team couldn't score goals and they couldn't stop other teams from scoring either. In May 1992, AS Cannes were relegated back to Ligue 2.

'What do I do now?' Zinedine said to his dad. He had worked so hard and now his career was in danger. He was very grateful to AS Cannes for helping him to develop as a young player but now he had to move on to bigger things. 'I don't want to play in the second division again!'

Smaïl could see how disappointed his son was but he wasn't worried. 'I'm sure that a first division club will try to sign you. You're far too good to go down!'

Fortunately, his dad was right. Several Ligue 1 clubs were interested in signing Zinedine, including his hometown team and league champions, Olympique de Marseille. They were building a great team with young French stars like Didier Deschamps and Marcel Desailly.

'That's my dream!' he told his brothers excitedly. 'I want to come home and win lots of trophies.'

In the end, however, Marseille decided not to make an offer. When he heard the news, Zinedine was very

upset. Luckily, FC Girondins de Bordeaux decided
to sign him instead. They weren't as successful as
Marseille but they were in Ligue 1 and they had
lots of talented young French players too. Zinedine
already knew their attacker Christophe Dugarry,
whom everyone called Duga, from the national
Under-18s team.

'Welcome to the real South of France!' Christophe
said happily when they met in pre-season training.
The sun was shining and Zinedine was sweating even
before he kicked a ball. 'Forget about Marseille – in a
year or two, we'll be better than them anyway.'

Bixente Lizarazu was the Bordeaux captain. He
was a clever, fast left-back and he played for the
French national team. Bixente made Zinedine feel at
home right from the start. The team worked hard but
they also laughed hard.

'Christophe, are you sure he's only nineteen?'
Bixente joked. 'I mean, look at his hair. Zinedine's
going bald already – he looks like a monk!'

On the football pitch, the three of them clicked
straight away. Bordeaux didn't have a main striker,

and so goals were a real team effort. The race to be the club's top scorer became very competitive. Christophe was the first to find the net and Bixente was next because he was the club's penalty taker.

But Zinedine, the Number 7, was full of self-belief. 'Just you wait until I start scoring,' he told them with a smile. 'You won't be able to stop me!'

Zinedine got his first goal against RC Lens in September 1992 and, by the end of January 1993, he had a total of seven. 'That's more than both of you put together!' he teased Christophe and Bixente.

The Bordeaux manager, Rolland Courbis, was delighted with his signing. With his help, Zinedine was staying calm on the pitch and creating lots of chances for the team. The goals were a very nice bonus.

'You've scored more for us in six months than you did in three years at Cannes!' Courbis said. 'What's got into you?'

'I've got good teammates!' Zinedine replied, putting his arm around Christophe Dugarry.

Courbis laughed. 'Zizou and Duga – what a partnership!'

Soon, everyone was calling them by their new nicknames. The team was having fun together both on and off the field. In the final weeks of the season, Bordeaux were battling to qualify for Europe.

'If we can finish fourth, we'll be in the UEFA Cup next year,' Duga said.

'Let's aim higher than that!' Bixente replied. 'PSG and Monaco are only a few points ahead of us. With you and Zizou in great form, we could even grab second place and play in the Champions League instead.'

The whole team was more motivated than ever. Bixente was right. With their star double act playing with so much confidence, there was nothing that Bordeaux couldn't achieve. Against FC Metz, Zizou got the first goal and Duga got the second. In their final match, the team was losing 2-1.

'Come on, we need to win to get fourth place!' Bixente shouted to his teammates. 'Let's give it one final push!'

His captain's team talk worked. Duga scored just before half-time and then Zizou got the winner. It was his tenth goal of an amazing breakthrough season.

'Europe, here we come!' they cheered together at the final whistle. After clapping and waving to their brilliant supporters, they headed back to the dressing room for more celebrations.

But there was even better news to come. When Marseille had their league title taken away, Bordeaux went up from fourth to third.

'Aren't you glad that you signed for us rather than Marseille now?' Courbis asked with a cheeky smile.

Zizou didn't need to answer that question. He was having the time of his life with Duga and Bixente at Bordeaux.

CHAPTER 13

FIRST STEPS WITH FRANCE

'Congratulations, Duga!' Zinedine cheered.

At the end of the 1993–94 season, his Bordeaux teammate had been called up to the France national team with Bixente. He was very pleased for Christophe but he couldn't help feeling a little jealous.

'Thanks, Zizou – you'll be joining us in no time!' his teammate replied.

Zinedine really hoped that was true. Bordeaux had finished joint third in Ligue 1 and he had been one of their star players again. With more strikers in the squad, he had been able to focus on what he did best – playmaking. He didn't score as many goals but he was even more important to the team.

'Even I got more than you this season!' Bixente joked.

'But how many of those goals were thanks to me?' Zinedine joked back.

Each time he collected the ball in midfield, he looked up for options in front of him. A run down the right wing? A run down the left wing? A through-ball to the strikers? A dribble towards goal? Whatever the options, Zinedine almost always made the right decision. That's why he was awarded the French Young Player of the Year award. It was a great honour to win the trophy but when would he get his first French cap? Like most twenty-two-year-olds, he was very impatient.

In August 1994, the national team played a friendly against the Czech Republic. After missing out on the 1994 World Cup, France were determined to make it to the Euro 1996 tournament in England. And their manager Aimé Jacquet wanted to make sure he had his best team ready for the qualifiers.

'Do you think there's any chance that I'll be in the squad?' Zinedine asked his teammates. 'The match is here in Bordeaux at the Stade Chaban-Delmas!'

'Yes! Don't worry, I've been telling everyone how good you are,' Christophe told him.

'Jacquet and his coaches have been watching you for months,' Bixente added. 'Don't get your hopes up but I think you've got a really good chance.'

Zinedine had never felt as nervous as he did on the day that the team was announced. But finally, he got the phone call that he was waiting for. He was in!

'Congratulations, Zizou!' Christophe cheered.

Zinedine was really pleased but he knew that it was just the first step. Next, he needed to show Jacquet that he deserved to play in the match. At the training camp, he worked harder than ever. He wasn't a young prospect anymore; he was a confident professional.

'Slow down, Zizou!' Bixente laughed. 'Leave some energy for the actual game.'

Christophe was named in the starting line-up, and Zinedine and Bixente were both on the bench. Zinedine was a little disappointed but there would still be plenty of time to shine. At the end of a boring first half, the Czech Republic scored two quick goals. Jacquet was furious – he needed to make changes quickly. He turned to his substitutes.

'Get warmed up!' he called out to Bixente.

Zinedine hoped that he would be next and after sixty minutes, he got his wish. With the adrenaline pumping all around his body, Zinedine felt amazing and unstoppable. He was about to make his international debut, and at home in the Bordeaux stadium! He tucked his Number 14 shirt into his shorts and waited for Corentin Martins to come off.

'Good luck!' Corentin said as they high-fived.

It was the proudest moment of his life as Zinedine ran out on to the pitch. He was determined to make a big impact and his shirt didn't stay tucked in for long. Soon, he was using it to wipe the sweat from his face. He didn't stop running from box to box, trying to create goals for France at one end and trying to stop their Czech opponents from scoring at the other.

With five minutes to go, Laurent Blanc played a great pass to Zinedine just inside the opposition half. He ran forward at top speed and dribbled past the first defender with ease. As the next defender ran in, Zinedine dragged the ball back, shifted it to his left foot and took a long-range shot. The ball swerved powerfully past the goalkeeper and into the bottom corner.

Goooooooooooooooooooaaaaaaaaaaaaaaaalllllllllllllll lllllllllll!!!!!!!!!!!!!!!!!!

Zinedine was delighted with his debut wondergoal but there was no time to celebrate. Bixente congratulated him as they ran back for the restart. 'We've got time to score another!' he shouted.

In the last few minutes, France won a corner. Jocelyn Angloma curled the ball into the penalty area and it was coming towards Zinedine. There wasn't much pace on the cross and he was still ten yards from goal. He needed to use all of his height, plus the technique that Jean Varraud had taught him at AS Cannes.

Zinedine leapt high into the air and used his neck muscles to power the ball towards goal. It flew like a rocket over the goalkeeper's arms and just under the crossbar.

Goooooooooooooooooooooaaaaaaaaaaaaaaaalllllllll llllllllllll!!!!!!!!!!!!!!

This time, the celebrations lasted a little longer. The fans waved their red, white and blue flags in the air and the players ran over to hug Zinedine.

'We've got time to score another!' Bixente shouted again, but Zinedine had used up all his magic for one day. A 2-2 draw would have to do. He had certainly made a big impact.

'What a debut!' Jacquet said, giving him a big pat on the back. 'It's like you've been playing international football for years!'

Zinedine thanked his manager for his kind words. That was his dream – to play international football for years to come.

CHAPTER 14

EUROPEAN ADVENTURES

After his amazing debut against the Czech Republic, Zinedine was the talk of France. He was young, he was strong, he could dribble, he could pass and he could score goals with either foot and with his head too. What more could you want?

When Manchester United's Eric Cantona was suspended for eight months, Jacquet dropped him from the national team and made Zinedine his number one playmaker. Zinedine was delighted. All of his hard work and patience was really paying off.

'I couldn't have done this without you guys!' he said to Christophe and Bixente.

Duga laughed. 'Yes, you're right about that!'

Playing together for both club and country was so much fun. Bordeaux weren't doing quite so well in Ligue 1 but Zinedine was enjoying the team's adventures in Europe. He was playing well and scoring goals but Bordeaux hadn't yet made it past the third round of the UEFA Cup. The following year, they were back to try again.

'This year, we're going to do much better,' Zinedine said confidently. 'We just have to believe in ourselves. We can beat anyone!'

Bordeaux started with comfortable victories over Vardar of Macedonia and Rotor Volgograd of Russia. Zinedine didn't score but he created lots of chances for his teammates. In the third round, they faced Spanish side Real Betis.

'Right, we need to step up our game now,' Bixente told the players ahead of the home leg. 'Betis are a very difficult team to beat. We need to be at our best!'

The rain poured down all game long but that didn't stop Zinedine. He was a proud father now and he wanted to celebrate his son Enzo's birth in style. He was at the centre of everything. In the first half, he received the ball in midfield and spread it wide to Bixente on the left wing. Bixente passed back to Zinedine, who was now on the edge of the penalty area. Instead of shooting, he played a first-time ball to Daniel Dutuel. Daniel shot past the keeper to make to finish off a great team goal. At the final whistle, Bordeaux had a 2-0 lead to take to Spain.

'We've still got a lot of work to do,' the manager, Slavoljub Muslin, told them. 'But if we can get an away goal, it will make a huge difference.'

Three minutes into the match, striker Anthony Bancarel headed a goal-kick down into Zinedine's path. He was at least forty yards from goal but he could see that the goalkeeper was off his line. It was definitely worth a try, especially with Zizou's amazing technique. He watched the ball carefully onto his weaker left foot and struck it as hard as he could. As it flew through the air, the Bordeaux fans held their breath.

Zinedine had hit the ball perfectly. The goalkeeper

sprinted backwards to make the save but it was too late. He could only touch it with his fingertips and push the ball into the net.

Goooooooooooooooooooooooooaaaaaaaaaaaaaaaaa allllllllllllllllllllllll!!!!!!!!!!!!

Zinedine had produced another moment of magic to take his team through to the quarter-finals. It was definitely the best goal that he had ever scored. He pumped his fists at the crowd as his teammates chased over to congratulate him.

'That's the best away goal I've ever seen!' Daniel cheered happily.

Zinedine's brilliant European performances were attracting lots of attention. In England, Blackburn and Newcastle were both preparing summer offers for him. He was pleased to hear that top clubs were interested in him, but he was fully focused on winning the UEFA Cup.

'We can talk about things at the end of May,' he told his agent.

In the quarter-finals, Bordeaux were up against Italian giants AC Milan. When they lost the away leg

2-0, some of the players feared that the dream might be over. But not Zinedine.

'We've just got to score three at home!' he said, as if that was the easiest thing in the world.

After fifteen minutes, Bixente crossed the ball into the box and Didier Tholot scored. 2-1! Suddenly, the Bordeaux players believed that they could pull off an amazing comeback.

In the second half, Bordeaux won a free-kick on the left. As he waited to take it, Zinedine wiped the sweat from his face with his sleeve, and concentrated. Christophe was calling for it in the penalty area and he needed to get his cross exactly right.

Zinedine curled the free-kick perfectly around the wall but it hit the referee! The ball bounced straight to Christophe, who turned and scored. 2-2!

'Great assist!' Christophe shouted as they celebrated.

'Thanks,' Zizou replied.

'No, I was talking to the referee!' Duga joked.

Zinedine wasn't finished yet. He dribbled forward from his own half and tried to play a great through-

ball. The defender blocked it but it came back towards Zinedine. He stretched out his leg and tapped it to Christophe. Christophe ran into the penalty area and smashed a shot into the top corner. 3-2 to Bordeaux!

Duga was a man on a mission. He ran straight to the creator of the goal, pointing and smiling. He gave Zizou a big hug and a kiss on the cheek.

'We did it!' Christophe cheered.

'We haven't done it yet,' Bixente reminded the team. 'There are still twenty minutes to go!'

They held on for a famous victory and a place in the semi-finals. Barcelona and Bayern Munich were both still in the tournament but Bordeaux were drawn against Slavia Prague.

'Zizou, you love playing against the Czechs!' Duga laughed.

He was right. As Zinedine dribbled into the penalty area, two defenders ran to tackle him. That left Christophe in lots of space and Zinedine had spotted him. He cut inside and poked the ball to Christophe for a simple tap-in. 1-0!

With two 1-0 wins, Bordeaux were into the UEFA
Cup final against Bayern Munich. A tough tie became
even tougher when Zinedine was ruled out of the first
leg and, without their superstar, Bordeaux lost 2-0.

'It's not over yet!' Zinedine told his teammates.
There was still the second leg. 'Remember that AC
Milan match?'

Zizou was back in the team for the second leg and
he worked hard but, unfortunately, there were no
moments of magic this time, and they lost again –
this time, 3-1. As Bayern lifted the trophy, Zinedine
couldn't help feeling disappointed but he was also
very proud of what Bordeaux had achieved.

'It's decision time now,' his agent told him soon
afterwards. Zinedine had won the 1996 Ligue 1
Player of the Year award and lots of clubs were
interested in signing him. 'Do you want to stay here
or go and play for Juventus?'

The chance to sign for the winners of the
Champions League, the best team in Europe?
Zinedine said yes.

CHAPTER 15

JOY AND DESPAIR AT JUVENTUS

Zinedine wasn't the first Frenchman to play for Juventus. One of his childhood heroes, Michel Platini, had played for the Italian team for five years in the 1980s and, now, Zinedine was joining his national teammate Didier Deschamps in the club's midfield.

There were lots of other French players in Serie A too. Lilian Thuram was playing for Parma, Youri Djorkaeff and Jocelyn Angloma were at Inter Milan, and Marcel Desailly was at AC Milan. Soon, another Frenchman would be on the move.

'Well, I couldn't let you go to Italy without me!' Duga said to Zizou. He had just signed for AC Milan.

'It's only a two-hour drive from Milan to Turin. We can see each other every week!'

Zinedine was very happy to hear that news. He could really do with having his best friend around. Italian football was proving a real shock after years in France. When Zinedine arrived for his first day of training, the Juventus manager Marcello Lippi took one look at him and sent him off to work with the fitness coach.

'Bring him back when he's added a few kilograms of muscle,' Lippi ordered.

For three weeks, Zinedine ran and ran and ran. It was the most painful experience of his life but he could feel himself getting fitter and fitter. Finally, the coach decided that Zinedine was ready to play football.

'Just in time for our first league match of the season!' Zinedine told his dad, sounding very relieved.

In the Number 21 shirt, he started the match against Reggiana alongside Didier in central midfield. With Didier doing most of the defensive work,

Zinedine tried to get forward as much as possible to create chances for the strikers. In the seventh minute, the ball came to him about thirty yards from goal. Out of the corner of his eye, he saw a defender approaching quickly.

Zinedine didn't have time to take a touch, but he had his X-ray football vision to help him. He slid a brilliant through-ball into the path of Alen Bokšić, who crossed to Christian Vieri. They went ahead, 1-0!

'What a start!' Alen cheered as he thanked Zinedine for the pass.

Thanks to his extra fitness work, Zinedine was coping well with the physical challenge of Italian football. He couldn't wait for the first important battle of the year – Juventus vs Inter Milan.

'The fans seem to like me but I want them to *love* me,' Zinedine said to Didier before kick-off.

'Well if you score your first Juve goal against Inter, you'll be an instant hero!' his teammate told him.

The atmosphere in the Stadio delle Alpi was incredible. Three-quarters of the stadium was completely covered in black and white and there wasn't a spare seat anywhere. The pressure was on but Zinedine loved the big games.

From the first minute, he was on fire. He twisted and turned his way into the penalty area and passed to Alen but he couldn't hit the target.

'Unlucky, next time!' Zinedine shouted.

A few minutes later, he curled a free-kick just over the crossbar. Juventus were getting closer and closer. Just before half-time, Vladimir Jugovi made it 1-0. The players celebrated happily but they knew that the game wasn't over. Inter would fight back.

'Let's get a second goal!' Ciro Ferrara called from defence.

After sixty minutes, a corner kick bounced out to Zinedine on the edge of the penalty area. He controlled the ball perfectly, looked up and curled a powerful shot through a gap in the defence. The ball dipped as it flew past the goalkeeper and into the bottom corner.

Goooooooooooooooooaaaaaaaaaaaaaaaaaaaaalllllllllll llllllllllllllllllll!!!!!!!!!!!!!

Zinedine had done it – he had scored his first

Juventus goal and what a goal it was! He ran to the
bench to celebrate with the substitutes. It was a
moment that he would never forget.

'How did you make that look so easy?' Alen asked,
but Zinedine could only shrug. He couldn't explain it.
It was natural talent.

Zinedine's first season in Italy was going brilliantly.
He scored a free-kick against Bologna and a penalty in
an amazing 6-1 win away at AC Milan.

'We just thrashed last year's Serie A Champions!'
Ciro screamed, giving Zinedine a big bear hug. 'The
title is going to be ours this time!'

Juventus were heading towards an Italian League
and Champions League double, and Zinedine was
loving every minute of it. In the Champions League
semi-final, the Ajax midfielders chased around after
him all game long but he was just too good for them.
Every touch, every pass, every dribble was clever and
perfect. After four assists, Zinedine finished it off with
a goal of his own.

'Wow, what a masterclass!' Lippi said after the final
whistle. Every fan in the stadium was up on their feet

to clap. The Juventus manager hardly ever smiled, but Zinedine's performance was worth it.

Smaïl and Malika were delighted for their son. 'This time last year, you were playing in the UEFA Cup Final and now you're in the Champions League final – that's what I call rapid progress!'

Their opponents in the final in May 1997 were German side Borussia Dortmund. Juventus were the favourites but it was going to be a very difficult match.

'They beat Manchester United, so they must be good,' Lippi told his players. 'Just because we won this competition last year, doesn't mean we're going to win it again. No team has ever won two years in a row. But if we play our best football, we have the chance to make history!'

As the Champions League anthem played, Zinedine looked up at the 60,000 fans in the Olympiastadion in Munich. He didn't usually get nervous but this was the biggest game of his young life. At the top of the Juventus midfield diamond, the strikers were relying on him to set up chances. Zinedine couldn't let his team down.

But Dortmund were ready to stop him. Everywhere Zinedine went, their midfielders Paul Lambert and Paulo Sousa went too, like a pair of shadows. Without the space to create his magic, Zinedine grew more and more frustrated. When Dortmund scored two quick goals, Juventus were in real trouble.

'What did I tell you?' Lippi shouted angrily at half-time. 'We're playing badly and they're beating us! If we don't score early in the second half, it's over.'

After sixty minutes, Alen passed to Zinedine and he finally had a tiny bit of space on the ball. He played a brilliant pass back to Alen for the one-two and he crossed for Alessandro Del Piero to score. 2-1!

But just when Juventus looked like they were back in the game, Dortmund scored again. The match was over and Zinedine felt like he had failed.

'That wasn't your fault,' Lippi told him as he sat on the grass after the final whistle. 'We win as a team and we lose as a team.'

Zinedine was grateful for his manager's support but he was too disappointed to reply. It was his most painful defeat ever.

Zinedine did, at least, win his first Serie A title with Bordeaux that season. It was very nice to finish his impressive debut season in Italy with a winner's medal. He joined in the big celebrations but he couldn't stop thinking about the winner's medal that he didn't have.

'We have to get to the Champions League final again next season,' he told Didier, 'and, this time, we have to win it!'

CHAPTER 16

WORLD CUP 1998: THE ROAD TO ANOTHER FINAL

'I can't believe it,' Zinedine muttered, staring down at the pitch in the Netherlands' Amsterdam Arena. 'I must be cursed!'

In 1996, he had lost in the UEFA Cup Final and, in 1997, he had lost in the Champions League Final. In 1998, Juventus made it all the way back to the Champions League final, just like Zinedine had told Didier that they would. With new signings Filippo Inzaghi in attack and Edgar Davids in midfield, they felt confident about beating Real Madrid.

'We're a better team this year,' Lippi told his players before kick-off. 'Be confident! Go out there and show Real that we can win the big games.'

Zinedine really hoped that his luck was about to change but it didn't. He worked hard to create chances for Alessandro and Filippo but, in the end, Predrag Mijatović scored the only goal of the game. Juventus and Zinedine had lost another major European final.

'I'm trying really hard to be a big-game player,' he moaned to Didier, 'but it's just not working!'

'Don't be so hard on yourself,' his teammate replied. 'In two years, you've won two Serie A titles and you've reached two Champions League finals – not many players can say that. Cheer up because, in a few weeks, we've got a World Cup to win!'

After losing to the Czech Republic in the semi-finals of Euro 1996, France were looking to go one better this time and reach the final. They were the hosts for the 1998 tournament and the whole nation had gone football crazy.

'Can you imagine the party if we win!' Zinedine said to Lilian Thuram with a smile. The streets of Paris were full of people and full of colour – the blue of France but also the colours of the other thirty-two countries.

Zinedine couldn't wait to play in such a big, international event. He had grown up watching the 1982 tournament on TV and now, sixteen years later, he was actually taking part. Brazil were the favourites to win but he knew that his team would be difficult to beat, especially on home soil. Brazil had the individual talent of Ronaldo and Rivaldo but France had the individual talent of Zinedine, *plus* great teamwork and team spirit.

Their defence was very strong – Fabien Barthez in goal, Lilian at right-back, Zizou's old friend Bixente at left-back, and Marcel Desailly and Laurent Blanc in the middle. In front of them, captain Didier was always in the right place at the right time to stop attacks.

'We'll keep the goals out,' Bixente laughed, 'but you'll have to get them *in* at the other end!'

In attack, Zinedine played with Youri Djorkaeff and Thierry Henry. Zinedine had the technique and vision, Youri had the skill and Thierry had the blistering pace. The only thing missing was a real goalscorer. France had a few strikers fighting for the starting spot, including one of Zinedine's best friends.

'Remember Duga and Zizou – Jacquet has to pick me!' Christophe joked as the squad prepared for the first match against South Africa. It was taking place at the Stade Vélodrome in Marseille, Zinedine's hometown. Smaïl was usually too nervous to watch his son play live, but this was a very special moment for the Zidane family.

'We wouldn't miss it for the world!' he told Zinedine proudly.

Christophe came on to replace Stéphane Guivarc'h early in the game. As he ran on, he winked at Zinedine – it was time for more Duga and Zizou. Zinedine dribbled forward and played a great pass to Christophe. He was through on goal but the keeper ran out and made a great save.

'Next time, I'll score,' Christophe said confidently.

Five minutes later, Zinedine curled a corner right onto Christophe's head. He flicked the ball into the far corner. 1-0!

'Thanks, mate!' he shouted to Zinedine, but it was drowned out by the noise in the stadium.

The match finished 3-0 and the French manager, Jacquet, was pleased with his team's start. 'If we can beat Saudi Arabia, we'll make it through to the second round,' he told the players.

In the Saudi Arabia game, Bixente ran down the left wing, passed to Zinedine and then kept running for the one-two. It was a move that they had used so many times at Bordeaux. Bixente crossed into the box and Thierry scored a tap-in. 1-0!

The French fans roared and the players ran in for a team hug. They were playing really well together.

In the second half, France were 2-0 up and cruising to victory. But as Zinedine went in for a tackle, he lost his temper. He won the ball but his foot came down on his opponent's leg. The referee was standing right next to the action and immediately showed Zinedine a red card. He was devastated.

'Why, what did I do?' he asked.

'You stamped on him,' the referee replied.

'No, I didn't mean to!' Zinedine argued, but it was no use.

As he walked off slowly, he felt really ashamed.

Jean Varraud at Cannes and Rolland Courbis at Bordeaux had spent so much time teaching him to stay calm on the pitch. He had let them down; he had let the whole of France down.

'We have to control ourselves,' Jacquet told the squad after the game, but he was mostly speaking to Zinedine. The manager was very disappointed in his star player.

Zinedine was suspended for the final group match against Denmark and the Round of 16 match against Paraguay. It was a nightmare watching his teammates as they struggled to create chances. They needed him but, because of one stupid foul, he wasn't there. Zinedine had definitely learnt his lesson. Luckily, Laurent Blanc scored the golden goal in extra-time.

'Well done, guys!' Zinedine said in the dressing room afterwards. 'I'll be back for the quarter-finals and I'll make up for my mistake, I promise.'

But after ninety minutes against Italy, it was 0-0 again. And after 120 minutes, it was still 0-0. Penalties!

'I'll go first,' Zinedine told Jacquet. He loved taking penalties.

He felt calm as he walked up and placed the ball on the spot. He stepped back and sent the goalkeeper the wrong way. Easy! As the ball hit the net, he raised his arms to the fans.

They were very happy to have him back. Bixente missed, but so did Demetrio Albertini. With the last spot-kick, Luigi Di Biagio hit the crossbar. France were through!

The French players celebrated the victory but Zinedine knew that they would need to do much better in the semi-finals. He needed to create more chances for the team.

Croatia were the surprise team of the tournament. Zinedine had played against their midfielders Zvonimir Boban and Aljoša Asanović in the Italian league. Their star striker, Davor Šuker, played for Real Madrid and he was the World Cup's top goalscorer.

'They beat Germany 3-0 in the last round,' Jacquet reminded them. 'We have to stay focused and start playing our best football.'

The match was at the Stade de France in Paris, in front of 76,000 supporters. Some of his teammates felt nervous but Zinedine was pumped full of adrenaline. He was ready to be the star. His first shot went straight at the keeper and his second was a spectacular volley that nearly went in the top corner.

'Keep going!' Didier shouted to him.

Šuker gave Croatia the lead but France didn't give up. A minute later, Lilian tackled Boban, played a one-two with Youri and scored. 1-1!

'Is that your first international goal?' Zinedine asked as they high-fived. Lilian nodded happily. 'Well, your timing was perfect!'

Twenty minutes later, Lilian did it again. With his left foot, he curled the ball into the bottom corner. 2-1!

'Wow, what's got into you today?' Didier laughed as they hugged their hero. 'You're on a hat-trick in a World Cup semi-final!'

Lilian didn't get his hat-trick but France got their victory. Zinedine was through to yet another final and, this time, he was going to win.

CHAPTER 17

WORLD CUP 1998: THE FINAL

'When I first arrived from Algeria, I worked in Saint Denis, right next to the Stade de France,' Smaïl told Zinedine as he prepared for the biggest match of his life. 'Now, nearly forty years later, my son is playing for France in a World Cup Final at the stadium – how amazing is that!'

There were lots of similar success stories in the squad. Like Zinedine, Youri and Thierry had been born in France but their parents were from other countries. Meanwhile, Marcel had been born in Ghana, Lilian in Guadeloupe, and Patrick Vieira in Senegal. This was the new France, where people from all over the world could come together and improve their lives. Zinedine was proud to be part of what people were calling a 'Rainbow nation'.

'Let's give our people something to really celebrate!' Lilian cheered.

Their opponents in the final were Brazil. With Ronaldo and Rivaldo in great form, Brazil were the favourites to win their fifth World Cup trophy. But behind the scenes, there was drama. Ronaldo wasn't well. At first he wasn't even named in Brazil's line-up but, in the end, he started the match anyway.

France just focused on their own game. As the players walked out onto the pitch, they looked up at a sea of blue, white and red. Zinedine took in the amazing atmosphere and breathed deeply. This was it. He had played well in the tournament but he hadn't scored and he hadn't been a matchwinner. There was just one game left to shine.

'Come on!' he clapped.

While Brazil's superstar looked weak and slow, France's superstar was on fire. From the very first minute, Zinedine controlled the game with his vision and skill. He linked midfield with attack, dribbling forward until he could see a good passing option in front of him. The Brazilian defence looked nervous and so Zinedine moved higher up the pitch. He had never felt so confident and powerful. Every touch was perfect.

'We need to take advantage and score!' he told Youri.

Zinedine often took the corners but not this time. 'You take it,' he told Emmanuel Petit. He was ready to score with a header, just like he had against the Czech Republic on his international debut.

Zinedine waited on the edge of the penalty area and made a late run towards the front post. Emmanuel's cross was perfect. Zinedine jumped high and headed the ball powerfully down into the bottom corner.

Goooooooooooooooooooooaaaaaaaaaaaaaaaaalllllllll llllllllllllll!!!!!!!!!!!!!

The whole of France went wild. He had done it! Zinedine had scored in a World Cup Final, and with a header too.

'Thanks, Jean Varraud!' he thought to himself. He

had put his old coach's lessons into practice again and this time on the world's biggest stage.

Zinedine ran to the fans and pumped his fist. As his teammates joined him, he roared and bumped chests with them. He was in the mood for more.

Just before half-time, Youri took a corner from the left. Again, Zinedine made a brilliant late run towards the six-yard box and headed the ball into the net.

Goooooooooooooooooaaaaaaaaaaaaaaaaaaaaaalllllllll llllllllllll!!!!!!!!!!!!!!

Zinedine was definitely a matchwinner now. He lifted his shirt to his face and kissed it again and again. He found Youri and they fell to their knees and hugged. Finally, Zinedine allowed himself to smile. He was playing the best game of his career.

In the crowd, his childhood hero Michel Platini clapped loudly. He had helped his country to win Euro 1984 but never a World Cup. Zinedine was on the verge of French history.

'We deserve this lead but the match isn't over yet,' Jacquet told his team. 'Another forty-five minutes of great football and we'll be World Champions!'

What France needed in the second half was a calm player who could pass the ball around and keep it in possession. Zinedine was that player. He slowed the game down and kept things simple. In injury time, Christophe passed to Patrick, who passed through to Emmanuel. Emmanuel placed his shot right in the corner of the net. 3-0!

At the final whistle, Zinedine thanked the referee and then the celebrations began. He hugged his old Bordeaux teammates Christophe and Bixente, his Juventus teammate Didier, his France teammates Youri, Lilian and Thierry. Zinedine was at the centre of a huge team hug and soon they were jumping up and down and singing. They were all friends and together they had won the World Cup for France. It didn't get any better than that.

'You finally won a final!' Didier teased Zinedine. 'How does it feel?'

'Absolutely amazing!' he replied. It still felt like a dream.

The winner's medal looked and felt wonderful around Zinedine's neck and the Man of the Match award made it even better. As Didier lifted the trophy into the air, everyone cheered – the players, the coaches, the fans in the stadium, the fans in Paris, the fans in Marseille and everywhere else in France. It was an amazing moment that no-one would ever forget. A victory for everyone in the Rainbow nation.

Zinedine waited for his turn – first Laurent, then Marcel, then him. He kissed the beautiful gold trophy and raised it up above his head. The fans gave him the loudest cheer of all. His face hurt from all the laughing and smiling.

As they did a victory lap around the pitch with the trophy, Zinedine thought back to his childhood days in La Castellane. They had all dreamed of winning the World Cup for France and now he had actually done it. Perhaps some of his old friends were there in the crowd, chanting his name.

'We might as well retire now,' Lilian joked. 'We're national heroes – what else is there to achieve?'

Zinedine disagreed. 'First there's the Champions League, then Euro 2000, then World Cup 2002...'

The list went on and on.

CHAPTER 18

BACK DOWN TO EARTH

The next few weeks were the craziest of Zinedine's
life. Thousands of fans filled the streets of Paris
to cheer as the players went past on their big bus
parade. And Zinedine's face was projected onto one
of France's most famous monuments, the Arc de
Triomphe.

'I can't believe this!' he told his brothers.

Once the World Cup celebrations were over,
Zinedine returned to Italy with Didier and Juventus's
big new signing, Thierry. After all of the excitement
and praise back in France, it was difficult to return
to normal. Zinedine was exhausted from the busy
summer and now there was lots of extra pressure on

him. He had become an international superstar but he still had to prove himself at club level.

'Defences are going to target you more than ever this season,' Edgar Davids warned him. 'You're the best player in the world now!'

In Juventus's first Serie A match of the 1998–99 season, against Perugia, Zinedine started well but his left knee didn't feel right. He tried to shake it off and ignore the pain but it was just getting worse. After only twenty-five minutes, he limped off the pitch, shaking his head with frustration.

'You needed a rest anyway!' Véronique told him as she made him comfortable on the sofa at home.

'One week off would have been okay, but three is too long,' Zinedine replied grumpily. He wasn't used to watching his teammates from the sidelines. He desperately wanted to be out on the pitch playing with them.

When he returned from injury, it took a long time to rediscover his form and fitness. At first, his feet didn't move as quickly and naturally as they had before and defenders double-marked him out of games. He drifted around the field, desperately looking for space.

'You're trying *too* hard,' Lippi told him in training. 'Just play your natural game and your confidence will return.'

As Zinedine struggled, so did Juventus. The team went six games without a league win and their title hopes were over by December. Only the Champions League was left but that looked very unlikely.

'I wish we could rewind and start the season again!' Zinedine complained.

During the difficult times, he still received two very welcome Christmas presents: the FIFA World Player of the Year and Ballon d'Or awards. It was now official – he really was the best player in the world. In 1998, he had been better than Šuker and better than Ronaldo. It was a very proud moment indeed. He returned to Paris and wore a smart suit for the Ballon d'Or ceremony. The big golden ball felt heavy in his hands but he held it happily as the media took photo after photo.

'It's time to get back to the football,' Zinedine then

told himself. He was glad that it was all over.

In February 1999, Carlo Ancelotti became the new manager of Juventus. His first job was getting the best out of Zinedine again.

'Forget 4-4-2!' Ancelotti told him in his office. 'From now on, I want you to play in behind the strikers. Didier and Edgar will do the defending. I want you to work just as hard as before but focus on attacking and creating. That's what we need from you.'

Zinedine loved his new free role. With his strength, technique and clever passing, he found more space and set up lots of goals for his teammates. He was starting to feel like his old self again. In the Champions League, Juventus beat Olympiakos to set up a semi-final against Manchester United.

'We're finding our form just in time!' Zinedine told Edgar. The Juventus midfield would have to be at its very best to compete against David Beckham, Ryan Giggs, Paul Scholes and Roy Keane.

At Old Trafford, Edgar, Didier, Zinedine and Antonio Conte battled very bravely. They knew that it was their last chance to win a trophy in the 1998–

99 season. Antonio scored in the first half but Giggs equalised in the last minute.

'Don't worry, that's a good result,' Didier said afterwards. 'We got an away goal and we can win back home at the Stadio delle Alpi.'

Thanks to Zinedine, Juventus got off to an incredible start. He was everywhere and Manchester United couldn't get the ball off him. When he was in central midfield, he looked up and played glorious long passes to the strikers. When he found himself on the left, he crossed the ball for Filippo to score at the back post. Five minutes later, Filippo scored again. 3-1 to Juventus!

'Stay calm and defend well,' Antonio shouted. He knew that Manchester United wouldn't give up.

But his teammates didn't listen. Keane scored to make it 3-2 and then Dwight Yorke made it 3-3 before half-time. United were ahead on away goals.

'Keep getting the ball to Zizou!' Ancelotti told his players. 'The Manchester United midfield can't get near him today. He'll create more magic.'

Zinedine kept making chances for his team but

nothing quite worked. Filippo missed some good chances, Jaap Stam made some good tackles and Peter Schmeichel made some good saves.

'Nearly – we'll score next time!' Zinedine shouted. He wasn't going to give up until the very end.

But with ten minutes to go, Andy Cole scored to make it 4-3 to Manchester United. Juventus were knocked out of the Champions League.

'We threw the game away!' Zinedine said angrily in the dressing room afterwards.

It was a very disappointing end to a very disappointing season for him. After winning the World Cup, Zinedine had hoped to continue his success with Juventus. But instead, they had finished seventh in Serie A, which meant the UEFA Cup rather than the Champions League.

'Do you want me to find you another club?' his agent asked him during the summer break. 'Real Madrid? Barcelona? Manchester United?'

Zinedine thought about it but, in the end, he decided to stay. 'I want to get Juventus back to the top again.'

With his help, Juventus finished second in the 1999–2000 Serie A season, just one point behind Lazio. It was frustrating to get so close to another league title but Zinedine was happy to be in the Champions League again. It was where he belonged.

Before that, however, it was time for Euro 2000 in Belgium and the Netherlands. Could Zinedine help France to win two international tournaments in a row?

CHAPTER 19

EURO 2000

France's Euro 2000 squad was almost exactly the same as the one for the 1998 World Cup. Zinedine couldn't wait to join up with his old friends to try to win another trophy for their country.

'Hello again!' Christophe cheered happily. 'Are you ready for this?'

Zinedine smiled and nodded. 'You bet I am!'

The only big changes for the French team were a new manager, Roger Lemerre, and two exciting new forwards – Bordeaux's Sylvain Wiltord and Real Madrid's Nicolas Anelka.

'We're going to get more goals this time,' Roger Lemerre told his players confidently as he looked around the dressing room before the first match against Denmark. With Youri, Zinedine, Thierry and Nicolas playing together in the same team, it seemed they would have no problem scoring.

Their manager was right – France won 3-0. Wearing the Number 10 shirt, Zinedine enjoyed his free role. When the Denmark defenders tried to rush him on the ball, he never panicked. Instead, he used his favourite trick, the 'Marseille Roulette'. With an elegant spin, he was in space again and ready to play a killer pass. His technique and vision helped to set up goals for Thierry and Sylvain.

'Great start, lads!' Lemerre said at the final whistle.

'We can do even better than that!' Zinedine said.

With a win over the Czech Republic, France qualified for the quarter-finals. When Zinedine was rested for the final group game against the Netherlands, his teammates really missed him. They lost 3-2.

'Don't worry – I'll be back to beat Spain!' Zinedine reassured them.

Not only did Zinedine return for that quarter-final

game, he came back at his classy best. He glided past the Spanish midfielders with ease, always looking for the attacking runs of Christophe, Thierry and Youri. He was controlling the game and no-one could touch him.

After half an hour, France won a free-kick just outside the penalty area. Zinedine was playing so well that he felt like he could do anything. He took a few steps back and curled the ball over the wall and into the top corner.

Goooooooooooooooooaaaaaaaaaaaaaaallllllllllllllllllll lllllll!!!!!!!!!!!!!!!!

As soon as he hit the free-kick, Zinedine knew that he had scored. He had kicked it with the perfect mix of accuracy and power. Scoring for his country was a great feeling but a brilliant goal in a top tournament? That was the best. He ran towards the fans and his best friends were right behind him.

'What a strike, Zizou!' Duga screamed.

'Another big game goal!' Bixente cheered.

Youri scored a brilliant second just before half-time. Spain tried and tried but they couldn't get past Marcel and Laurent, the rocks in defence. France were through to another semi-final.

'Two more performances like that and we'll win the trophy!' Lemerre encouraged his team. They were playing with lots of style and self-belief.

Portugal would be a difficult team to beat, however. They had a good defence and two brilliant midfielders, Rui Costa and Luis Figo. Zinedine knew how dangerous they could be, but he was determined to prove that he was even more dangerous.

After ninety minutes, the score was 1-1. Zinedine was desperate to do something special but Portugal were defending very well. His time would come. In the last few minutes, there was a handball in the box. Penalty to France!

Zinedine took a deep breath and looked up at the goal in front of him. From the penalty spot, it looked a long way away. 'It's easy,' Zinedine said to himself, 'you practise these every day in training.' When the pressure was on, he had nerves of steel. As the goalkeeper dived low to one side, Zinedine struck the ball into the top corner of the other side.

*Gooooooooooooooooooooaaaaaaaaaaaaaalllllllllllllllll
lllllllll!!!!!!!!!!!!!!!!!*

It was an unstoppable spot-kick. Zinedine ran
towards the bench with one arm raised in the
air and a huge smile on his face. He was France's
matchwinner yet again.

'That's the coolest penalty I've ever seen,' Lilian
told him. 'I knew that we could rely on you!'

Zinedine was already thinking ahead to the final.
He was so close to another winner's medal but Italy
would be their toughest opponents yet. Playing for
Juventus in Serie A, Zinedine knew all about their
national team. They had the best defence in the
world and enough great attackers to win the game.

'We have to be careful,' Lemerre warned them
before kick-off. 'They're a very clever side. If we make
mistakes, they will take advantage!'

That's exactly what they did. When Italy took the
lead, Zinedine's first thought was the curse.

'No, that's over!' he told himself. 'I won the World
Cup and now I'm going to win the Euros too.'

He kept battling and starting attacks for his

teammates, but time was running out. Zinedine feared the worst but in the last minute of injury time, Sylvain ran into the penalty area and shot under the goalkeeper and into the net. 1-1!

'Yes!' Zinedine shouted, giving Sylvain a big hug. 'Right, we need to score one more!'

But Zinedine was exhausted. Thankfully, the substitutes came to France's rescue. In extra time, Robert Pirès dribbled down the left wing and crossed into the box. David Trezeguet was there to smash the ball into the back of the net. 2-1! Golden Goal for France!

The stadium erupted into noise and Zinedine moved his tired legs as fast as possible to join the celebrations. They had done it together as a team.

'We're Champions of the World and now Champions of Europe too!' Christophe screamed up into the Rotterdam sky.

It had been an amazing few years for French football and Zinedine was delighted that he had played such a big role in its success. It was still hard to believe. A few years earlier, he had been a promising young player in France. Now, he had won the World Cup and Euro double, and he was both the Best Player at Euro 2000 and the FIFA World Player of the Year.

As Didier lifted the trophy, Zinedine was right at the centre of the team huddle. Golden confetti filled the air and they cheered loudly until they lost their voices. Zinedine wanted the night to go on forever.

CHAPTER 20

READY FOR REAL MADRID

After five good years in Italy, at Juventus, Zinedine decided that it was time to move on. He was about to turn twenty-nine and he wanted one more big challenge in his career. For most of the 1990s, Italy's Serie A had been the best league in Europe, but now the English Premier League and Spain's La Liga had taken over. Juventus had finished second in Serie A again and they had been knocked out of Europe in the first round.

'I can't retire without winning the Champions League,' Zinedine told his agent, 'and I'm not going to do it here.'

'In that case, how about Manchester United? Or

Bayern Munich? Or Real Madrid?'

Madrid was Zinedine's number one choice. Véronique wanted to move to a city with lots of culture and nice warm weather, and Zinedine wanted to win big trophies. Real Madrid was perfect for them both – a very rich club that really meant business. Being the Champions of Europe wasn't enough for them. They wanted to build a team of the best players in the world and money wasn't a problem. They had already signed Luis Figo for nearly £40million – could Zinedine be the next 'Galáctico'?

He hoped so, but Juventus weren't going to let him go easily.

'Zizou is not for sale,' the Italian club kept telling the media. 'He signed a five-year contract with us.'

'What are we going to do?' Zinedine asked his agent. He was determined to go to Madrid.

'We're going to wait for Real to make a really big offer that Juve can't refuse,' he replied.

Juventus certainly weren't going to let Zinedine go cheaply. They had signed him from Bordeaux for just £2.25million and they wanted to make lots of profit on selling their superstar. The offer that Juventus finally accepted was a massive £45.8million.

'That's a ridiculous amount of money to pay for one player!' Zinedine argued, although he was very relieved to know that the deal was going through.

'You're the most expensive player in the world,' his dad told him proudly.

'Now, you have to make sure that you're worth it!' his brothers teased him.

The Zidanes flew to Madrid on a private jet. 'Ah, that's better!' Véronique said, feeling the July sun on her face. It was like being back in the south of France again.

When Zinedine arrived, the best shirt numbers were already taken – Raúl was Number 7 and Luis was Number 10. The only available number between 1 and 11 was 5.

'I'll take it,' he said immediately.

'Are you sure?' the coaches asked. They wanted him to be happy. 'Normally defenders wear that shirt!'

Zinedine didn't care about things like that. Any

Real Madrid shirt would do. He just wanted to
be playing and winning. At the press conference,
Zinedine held up his white Number 5 and smiled for
the cameras. His Spanish wasn't very good yet, so he
spoke in French instead.

'It's a massive honour to sign for this great club,'
he told the thousands of fans who were watching on
TV. 'I've always wanted to come here and win lots of
trophies with Real Madrid.'

Zinedine, Luis, Raúl, Fernando Morientes and
Steve McManaman all in the same team – what could
go wrong? In training, they played amazing, exciting
football together, but it took a while for them to gel
in proper matches. They needed to get to know each
other and work together as a team.

'You'll have to chase back *sometimes*,' Claude
Makélélé, his French midfield partner told him. 'I
can't do everyone's defensive work all of the time!'

At first, playing for Real Madrid was a little
overwhelming for Zinedine. At Juventus, there
were never more than 50,000 fans in the Stadio
delle Alpi, but Real's Bernabéu stadium was always

full, with 75,000 fans watching him, cheering him, criticising him.

'I need to learn to block all of that out,' he told Véronique. 'I just need to focus on my game.'

In his third La Liga match against Real Betis, Zinedine received the ball from Raúl. He was in lots of space on the right side of the penalty area. It was a pretty easy finish but he wanted to make sure. He took a touch to control it and then shot past the keeper.

Goooooooooooooooooaaaaaaaaalllllllllllllllllllllll!!!!!!!!

'Welcome to the team!' Raúl shouted.

Zinedine was pleased to get his first goal but it wasn't enough. Real Madrid lost the match 3-1.

'We have to start winning games,' the manager Vicente del Bosque told his players. 'We've spent a lot of money on amazing players and right now, the fans aren't happy at all. The pressure is on!'

In the next match against Espanyol, Roberto Carlos passed to Raúl, who passed back to Zinedine. From just outside the box, he shot into the bottom corner.

Gooooooooooooaaaaaaaaaaaaaalllllllllllllllll!!!!!!!!!!!

'The Galácticos are go!' Zinedine shouted happily.

Roberto Carlos scored a stunning free-kick, Luis scored a penalty, Raúl scored a great team goal, and Steve scored a tap-in. The match finished 5-1.

'That's more like it!' Del Bosque said as he clapped his players off the pitch.

When they really worked together, the Galácticos were simply unstoppable.

Against Deportivo a few months later, Luis dribbled forward at speed and played a one-two with Raúl. On the edge of the penalty area, Luis passed across to Zinedine. He had one defender in front of him and three approaching fast. He dragged the ball away from the first defender, then moved the ball elegantly from one foot to the other and then back to his left foot. With his opponents totally bamboozled, he curled his shot past the goalkeeper.

Goooooooooaaaaaaaaaaaaaaaalllllllllllllllllllll!!!!!!!!!!

Zinedine ran to the Madrid fans as they chanted his name at the top of their voices. *Zizou! Zizou! Zizou!*

The Spanish newspapers called it a wondergoal. Zinedine was very happy with his new home.

CHAPTER 21

CHAMPIONS LEAGUE GLORY

Real Madrid finished the 2001–02 La Liga season behind Valencia and Deportivo, but two points ahead of arch rivals Barcelona. And Zinedine's biggest dream was still alive: a first Champions League trophy. Real Madrid were through to the final after impressive wins over Bayern Munich *and* Barcelona.

'This is my year!' Zinedine told his teammates confidently. '*Our* year!'

In the semi-final first leg at the Nou Camp, the 80,000 Barcelona fans booed them all game long. It was a difficult atmosphere to play in but Zinedine was focused on reaching another final. He wasn't the quickest player on the pitch but he sprinted after

Raúl's clever through-ball as fast as he could. The Real fans held their breath. An away goal could be vital.

With the Barcelona centre-back hot on his heels, Zinedine knew it was time to shoot. He looked up and saw that the goalkeeper was off his line. If anyone could get it right, Zizou could. As the defender dived in, Zinedine coolly chipped the ball towards goal. The keeper stretched up his arm but he could only deflect it into the net.

Goooooooooooooooooooooooaaaaaaaaaaaaaaaaaalllll lllllllllllllllllllll!!!!!!!!!

'That was so classy!' Roberto Carlos screamed, giving Zinedine a big hug. He had scored yet another important goal.

In the last minute, Steve scored another chip to make it 2-0.

'You're such a copycat!' Zinedine joked as they celebrated a brilliant victory.

Now they just needed to beat the German team Bayer Leverkusen in the final, but that wouldn't be easy. Real Madrid had the stars but Leverkusen had excellent players like Michael Ballack and Lúcio, and they were playing with lots of confidence.

'There's no such thing as favourites in a Champions League final,' Del Bosque told his players. 'In a single game, either team can win. If we play well, we'll win – it's that simple!'

On a cold, wet night at Glasgow's Hampden Park, Zinedine was determined to play well. It was his third final and this was his best chance yet to complete the big hat-trick. He already had the World Cup and the European Championships, but he wanted that Champions League trophy desperately. It would be a really special achievement.

In the eighth minute, Roberto Carlos launched a long throw towards the Leverkusen box. Raúl got to it first and steered it past the goalkeeper. 1-0!

'What a start!' Real Madrid's captain, Fernando Hierro, cheered.

But if they thought it was going to be an easy win, they were wrong. Lúcio equalised with a header five minutes later. Real Madrid needed another goal and Zinedine did his best to create it. He was dominating the midfield with his neat touches and long passes.

'Keep going,' Fernando told him, 'you're our big game player and we need you!'

Roberto Carlos played a great one-two down the left wing with Santiago Solari and then flicked a high ball over to Zinedine. As it fell from the sky, he thought about his options. Did he have enough time to control it first? No, a defender was chasing back, so he would have to hit it on the volley. He knew that he could get it right. He had the best technique in the world.

Zinedine swivelled his body and watched the ball carefully as he kicked it with his left foot. He caught it perfectly and the ball flew past the keeper and into the top corner.

Gooooooooooooooooooooooaaaaaaaaaaaaaaalllllllllllll llllllllllll!!!!!!!!!!!

What a magnificent strike! Zinedine ran along the side of the pitch, screaming with joy. Eventually his teammates caught him and jumped on top of him.

'That deserves to be the matchwinner!' Raúl said.

In the end, it *was* the winning goal. Zinedine would never forget the feeling when the referee blew the final whistle. His long wait for Champions League glory was over.

'We did it!' he told Santiago as they jumped up and down. 'I just can't believe it!'

It was one of the proudest moments of his career. With his winner's medal around his neck, Zinedine went up to join his teammates on the stage. As he looked for somewhere to stand, Steve shouted out:

'Zizou, you should be in the middle at the front. You were the man of the match!'

Zinedine stood behind Fernando and Raúl as they lifted the trophy. Shoots of fire rose from the stadium roof and music filled the air:

We are the Champions, My Friends,
And We'll Keep on Fighting Till the End

The Real Madrid players joined in with the singing. Zinedine did a lap of honour around the stadium, kissing the trophy and raising it high for everyone to see. He didn't ever want to let the trophy go. The fans cheered loudly as he walked past, and waved their purple and white scarves.

Zizou! Zizou! Zizou!

The fans loved him and he loved them back. They were the best supporters in the world.

'We made the right decision coming here!' Zinedine told Véronique happily.

'And they made the right decision to bring you here,' his wife replied. 'After that goal, £45.8million looks like a bargain!'

CHAPTER 22

THE GALÁCTICOS

'So who do you think will be our next Galáctico?' Luis asked in pre-season training.

'David Beckham?' Raúl suggested.

'Thierry Henry?' Zinedine guessed.

'No, I think it'll be Ronaldo,' Roberto Carlos said confidently.

Zinedine laughed. 'You're only saying that because you're both Brazilian!'

But Roberto Carlos was right – Ronaldo became Real Madrid's new star striker. Zinedine had played against him in Italy and, of course, in that amazing 1998 World Cup Final. He was very excited to now be playing together on the same team.

'With your pace and my passing, this is going to be so much fun!' he said happily.

Ronaldo made his debut as a substitute against Alavés in October 2002. The atmosphere was nice and relaxed in the dressing room before the match. 'Don't worry,' Zinedine said to his new teammate, 'I'll make sure that we're winning comfortably by the time you come on!'

In the very first minute, Zinedine ran into the penalty area. He cut inside on to his right foot, went past one tackle and curled an unbelievable shot into the top corner.

Goooooooooooooooooooooaaaaaaaaaaaaaalllllllllllll llllllll!!!!!!!!!!!!!!!

On the bench, Ronaldo clapped and smiled. 'Wow, I think I'm going to enjoy playing with these guys!' he said to himself. Finally, he came on after 64 minutes. A minute later, Roberto Carlos crossed the ball to him, whereupon the Brazilian chested the ball down and fired the ball past the keeper.

'Welcome to the team!' Zinedine shouted as he jumped on him.

The Galácticos were getting better and better. Zinedine and Luis were the creators and Ronaldo and Raúl were the scorers. It was a simple plan but it worked really well because they were the best players in the world.

'No-one ever talks about me!' Claude Makélélé moaned. He did a very important job for the team in defensive midfield. 'It's not fair. I do all the dirty work and you guys get all the glory!'

Zinedine was devastated when they lost to his old club Juventus in the Champions League semi-finals, but Real Madrid did at least win the Spanish league title for 2002–3.

'We're not the Champions of Europe this time, but we're the Champions of Spain. That still feels pretty amazing!' Zinedine said as he walked around the Bernabéu pitch with the La Liga trophy in his hands. He never got tired of winning.

'So who's going to be the next Galáctico?' Luis began again, ahead of the 2003–04 season.

'I still think Thierry,' Zinedine answered.

'And I still think Becks,' Raúl guessed.

'I'll go for Alessandro Nesta,' Ronaldo said.

'What, a defender?!' Luis laughed. 'Can a defender really be a Galáctico?'

'Of course!' Ronaldo replied. 'Roberto Carlos is a defender! We have lots of great attackers already. To be a great team, we need to have the best players in *every* position.'

Raúl was correct this time – David Beckham became Real Madrid's new star midfielder. Zinedine had played against Becks many times during his time at Manchester United. He had different skills that would be really useful for the team.

'Roberto Carlos, you better watch out!' Zinedine joked. 'There's a new free-kick king in town!'

Real Madrid's season got off to a great start. Against Racing Santander, Ronaldo chipped the ball to Zinedine on the edge of the penalty area, just like Roberto Carlos had done in the 2002 Champions League Final. The technique was really difficult but Zinedine knew that he could do it again. This time, he went for the right foot volley. He struck it sweetly and the ball flew past the keeper and into the net.

Goooooooooooooooooooooaaaaaaaaaaaaalllllllllllllllll lllll!!!!!!!!!!!!!!!

'That's a proper Galáctico goal!' Ronaldo cheered as the whole team celebrated together.

But soon they were battling against each other for a different prize – the World Player of the Year award. In 2001, Luis had won, with Becks second and Raúl third. Ronaldo had won it twice, and so had Zinedine, in 1998 and 2000. Who would be the first to get the hat-trick?

'You're four years younger than me,' Zinedine told Ronaldo as they arrived in Switzerland for the ceremony. 'You've got plenty of time to get your third trophy – time is running out for me!'

Ronaldo came third, and Arsenal's Thierry Henry came second. 'And the 2003 FIFA World Footballer of the Year is...' the presenter began, '...Zinedine Zidane!'

Zinedine couldn't stop smiling as he collected the trophy. Football's top players, coaches and journalists had picked him again as the best player in the world. He was Galáctico Number One.

'I am so proud to win this special award,' he said in his speech to the star-studded audience. 'Thank you all for voting for me!'

Real Madrid were in the La Liga title race right until the last few weeks. But at the crucial moment, they lost five out of six games and finished fourth.

'How did we throw it away so badly?!' Zinedine asked himself as the players sat in silence in the dressing room. Real Sociedad had just thrashed them 4-1 at the Bernabéu.

The Galácticos were learning an important lesson. You couldn't just bring the best players in the world together and expect to win everything. The most successful sides were built around great teamwork, not individual stars. And the most successful sides had good players all over the pitch, not just in attack.

'Let's hope the next Galácticos are defenders,' Zinedine said glumly.

Walter Samuel and Jonathan Woodgate helped to make Real Madrid a more balanced team for the 2004–5 season. With quality players at the back, they conceded fewer goals and Zinedine and co. could focus on creating chances and winning games.

The problem was that their arch rivals, Barcelona, were also winning games. With Ronaldinho, Samuel Eto'o and Deco, they were running away with the league.

'We have to stop them!' Zinedine told his teammates.

Barcelona won the first El Clásico match at the Nou Camp, but Real Madrid were determined to get revenge back at the Bernabéu. Early on, Ronaldo dribbled from the right wing into the box. As he looked up for the cross, Zinedine made a great run towards the back post. With a brilliant diving header, he scored.

Goooooooooaaaaaaaaaaaalllllllllllllllllllllllll!!!!!!!!!!!!!!

'Zizou, are you okay?' Roberto Carlos called out. To score, Zinedine had crashed into the goalpost.

He sat up slowly with a sore head. 'Ow, did I score?'

Ronaldo laughed. 'Yes, thanks to my great cross!'

When the Galácticos were at their best, no-one could stop them. Soon, Ronaldo scored from Becks' brilliant free-kick and Raúl scored from Roberto Carlos's pass.

'4-2 – what a win!' Raúl shouted at the final whistle. 'La Liga isn't over yet.'

Despite their hard work, Barcelona held on to win the league title. Zinedine was disappointed to end another season without a trophy. He really enjoyed playing for Real Madrid but, at the age of thirty-three, he was picking up more injuries than ever. It took him longer and longer to recover after each match.

And the Galáctico era was ending. Luis had been sold to Inter Milan, and bright young talents Sergio Ramos and Robinho had arrived. Zinedine was happy to help the new stars by sharing his big-game experience, but he didn't want to get in the way of the future.

'I'll see how I feel in a few months,' Zinedine told Véronique.

He played a lot of matches in the 2005–6 season, but he was getting more and more frustrated with himself.

'My body just won't let me play as well as I used to,' he complained to Ronaldo.

'What are you talking about?!' he replied. 'You're still as amazing as ever!'

There were still lots of moments of pure genius. Against Sevilla, Zinedine scored his first goal from the penalty spot and his second was a beautiful chip over the keeper. He had never scored a hat-trick before – this was his big chance! In the last minute, Becks passed to him in the penalty area. Some players would have got over-excited but not Zizou. He was as calm as ever. He chested the ball down, took his time and shot into the net with his left foot.

Goooooooooooooooooaaaaaaaaaaaaaaaalllllllllllllllllll llllllll!!!!!!!!!!!!!!!!

'I'm pretty sure that you've achieved everything in football now!' Becks joked as they celebrated.

His teammate was right. By April, Zinedine had made up his mind. He had won the Champions League and the Spanish League at Real Madrid but, now, it was time to go.

'I'm sorry but I can't carry on for another season,' Zinedine told the media. 'I've been thinking about it for a long time and this is my final decision.'

The Real Madrid players and fans were very upset. They loved playing with him and watching him play.

'There's no-one else like you, Zizou!' Raúl said with a sad smile. He would really miss his friend.

Zinedine's last game for Real Madrid was at the Bernabéu in May 2006 against Villarreal. The fans held up banners showing his face and his Number 5 shirt. They would never forget their hero. 'Thanks for the magic, Zizou!' they cheered loudly. Zinedine clapped the amazing supporters. He would never forget them either.

It was a very emotional day. In his final match, Zinedine gave yet another midfield masterclass. With his unique style and elegance, he glided around the pitch. His touch, his passing, his dribbling – everything was perfect. All that was missing was a goal.

In the second half, Becks dribbled down the right wing. Zinedine was there at the back post, waiting for a great cross. When it arrived, he didn't put lots of power on his header – Zizou was too clever and classy for that. Instead, he coolly placed a delicate header right in the far corner of the net.

*Goooooooooooooooooooaaaaaaaaaaaaaaaaaalllllllllllll
lllllllllll!!!!!!!!!!!!!!!*

'That was a thing of beauty!' Roberto Carlos
shouted, giving him a big hug. 'What a way to say
goodbye!'

When Zinedine came off with a few minutes to
go, the Real Madrid fans rose to their feet to applaud
him. After the game, he went back into the middle
of the pitch and waved with tears in his eyes. His
incredible club career was over but he wasn't leaving
Real Madrid behind. Zinedine's four sons, Enzo, Luca,
Théo and Elyaz, were all part of their youth team and
he hoped to start his coaching career there too.

But before that, Zinedine had one last trophy to
play for – the 2006 World Cup.

CHAPTER 23

WORLD CUP 2006

'I've thought long and hard about this and it's time to end my international career with France,' Zinedine had told the world back in 2004.

After their great achievements in 1998 and 2000, things had fallen apart. At the 2002 World Cup, Zinedine missed the first two games because he was injured. When he returned, it was too late: France were knocked out in the first round.

Two years later, Zinedine had led France to the quarter-finals of Euro 2004. He scored twice against England and once against Switzerland but he couldn't stop them losing to Greece. After that embarrassing defeat, Zinedine made his decision. The glory days were over. He was only thirty-two but France needed to start again with a brand-new team.

Unfortunately, their brand-new team didn't do so well. In the 2006 World Cup qualifiers, France drew matches against Israel, Republic of Ireland and Switzerland. All three games finished 0-0. Why couldn't France score? The manager, Raymond Domenech, knew exactly what was missing.

'I hope Zizou changes his mind,' he thought to himself.

One night, Zinedine lay awake, tossing and turning. It was very late but he couldn't sleep. All he could think about was France. Had he retired from international football too early? Could he still be a hero for his country? Eventually he called his brother, Nourredine.

'I want to play for France again,' he said.

By the end of 2005, Zinedine was back in the French team, along with Lilian and Claude. Their combined experience boosted the team's spirit and helped them to top their group.

'World Cup 2006, here we come!' the team cheered together.

Zinedine was excited about his big farewell in Germany. He had one last chance to shine on the international stage. He now had over one hundred caps for France and he was the captain.

'Let's make our nation proud!' he told the players.

France started slowly, with draws against Switzerland and South Korea, and they needed to win their last group match against Togo. And after two yellow cards, Zinedine was suspended. He had to watch from the sidelines as Patrick and Thierry scored the important goals.

'Well done, boys!' Zinedine said at the final whistle, giving everyone a hug. 'That's the first challenge completed.'

In the second round it became much more difficult, when they faced Spain. Their opponents took the lead but France didn't give up; Zinedine made sure of that. Franck Ribéry scored the equaliser and from Zinedine's free-kick, Patrick made it 2-1. In the last minute of the match, Zinedine was through on goal. He cut inside past the defender and sent the keeper the wrong way.

*Gooooooooooooooooooooaaaaaaaaaaaallllllllllllllllllll
llllll!!!!!!!!!!!!!!!!!!!!!*

Zinedine was delighted to get his name on the
scoresheet. It was a real captain's goal to secure the
victory.

'We can beat anyone!' he told his teammates
excitedly. He couldn't wait for the quarter-final.

But could they really beat Brazil? They had
Ronaldo, Kaká *and* Ronaldinho in their team, and
after the 1998 World Cup final, they were looking
for revenge. Zinedine knew exactly how dangerous
Ronaldo could be.

'We have to stay focused and play like a team,' he
told the players in the dressing room.

As the teams got ready for kick-off, Zinedine felt
relaxed and ready. He teased Ronaldo about beating
him again but, once the match started, Zinedine put
on his serious game-face. In the first minute he used
his strength to hold off two Brazilian midfielders and
then backheeled the ball cleverly between them. The
France fans loved his tricks.

Olé! Olé!

With a beautiful stepover, he glided past another Brazilian midfielder and kept running forward.

Olé! Olé!

Zinedine was ending his career in great style. He played like it was a casual training session, not an important World Cup quarter-final. He juggled the ball on his foot and did all sorts of tricks and flicks. Brazil just could not tackle him but France needed to score to win. He curled a free-kick right on to Florent Malouda's head, but his header went over the bar.

'Unlucky, keep going!' Zinedine shouted.

In the second half, he curled another ball into the box and, this time, Thierry volleyed the ball into the net. 1-0! France defended well and Brazil couldn't score. At the final whistle, Ronaldo came and hugged his friend.

'Congratulations, you were absolutely magnificent today!' he said. 'You've still got it – you can't give up now!'

Zinedine won the Man of the Match award. He was leading his country to glory yet again.

'Don't make this my last match!' he begged his

teammates ahead of the semi-final against Portugal.

A second World Cup final would be the perfect end to his amazing career. But first, he had to get past his old Real Madrid teammate Luis, and Cristiano Ronaldo.

Zinedine didn't play quite as well as he did against Brazil, but he scored the crucial goal. After half an hour, Thierry was fouled in the box. Penalty!

Zinedine had been taking penalties all his life. Pressure? What pressure? He only took one step back and then placed his shot right in the bottom corner. The goalkeeper dived the right way but he still couldn't save it.

Gooooooooooooooooaaaaaaaaaaalllllllllllllllllllll!!!!!!!!!

Zinedine roared up into the sky. Sixty minutes later, France were through to the World Cup final. He swapped shirts with Luis.

'What a legend!' Portugal's captain smiled. 'You're a delight to play with and a nightmare to play against. Football will miss you, Zizou. Good luck!'

France had just one more great team to beat – Italy, the team they had beaten in the Euro 2000 final.

Could they do it again? Zinedine was sure that his team could do it. 'We've done so well to get this far. One more push!' he cheered.

France took the lead early on, thanks to Zinedine. It was his coolest penalty ever. His *Panenka* chip went over the diving keeper, hit the crossbar and bounced down over the line.

Goooooooooooooaaaaaaalllllllllllllllllll!!!!!!!!!!!!!!!!!

He had done it again, another goal in a World Cup final. He was the ultimate big-game player.

'Our hero to the rescue!' Lilian joked as they celebrated.

But when Italy equalised, Zinedine couldn't produce any more of his magic. With every missed opportunity, he became more and more frustrated. He wanted to win and he wanted to be the hero. France needed their captain to stay calm but, in extra-time, he exploded with rage. Suddenly he was ten years old again and boys were calling him nasty names. Zinedine pushed Marco Materazzi's chest with his head and was sent off.

Without their leader, France lost the penalty shoot-out. It was a terrible way to end a terrific career.

'I have to ask for your forgiveness,' Zinedine told his nation. 'There are no excuses for what I did.'

And with that, Zizou retired from football. His amazing journey had taken him all the way from the estates of Marseille to the top of the game. He had won every major trophy – the World Cup, the Euros, the Champions League, Serie A, La Liga, the Ballon d'Or and the World Player of the Year award. And there were so many match-winning moments to remember.

No, he wasn't perfect but he *was* extraordinary. No-one had ever combined spirit with style like Zizou. He was one of a kind, with every skill to choose from; the killer pass, the beautiful dribble, the curling shot, the powerful header. And when the pressure was on, Zinedine had always raised his game to the highest level.

As Brazilian legend Pelé told the media: 'Zidane is the master. Over the past ten years, there's been no one like him, he has been the best player in the world.'

Turn the page for a sneak preview of
another brilliant football story by
Matt and Tom Oldfield. . .

PAUL POGBA

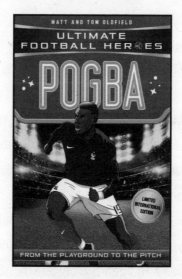

Available now!

CHAPTER 1

POGBACK

'This is a must-win match,' José Mourinho told his Manchester United team before their home game against Premier League champions Leicester City. 'Today, we need our leaders to lead.'

Paul knew that he was one of the leaders that Mourinho was talking about. His £89million return to Old Trafford had been the biggest transfer story of summer 2016. The '#PogBack' campaign had taken over the Twittersphere and thousands of fans bought his '6 POGBA' shirt and copied his cool tricks and hairstyles.

After moving to play for Juventus at the age of eighteen, four years later Paul was back at

Manchester United. The French player had established himself as an international superstar and a four-time Italian league winner. Expectations were very high. Ever since Paul Scholes' retirement, United had been seeking a match-winning midfielder and Paul fitted the bill: a box-to-box midfielder who could tackle, dribble and shoot. He was part-Patrick Vieira, part-Zinedine Zidane and part-Ronaldinho, and he would bring glory days back to Old Trafford. That was Mourinho's big plan when he took over as manager.

But after a great start to the new season against Southampton, United had lost two matches in a row to local rivals Manchester City and then to Watford. Lots of people were already criticising Paul. Was he really as good as people said he was? Why wasn't he controlling games? Why hadn't he scored any goals? Why had United paid so much money for him?

'Don't listen to the negative comments,' his mum, Yeo, told him. She was a very important part of Paul's life, offering advice and support when he needed it most. 'We all know how good you are!'

English football was much faster and more physical than Italian football. Paul needed time to adapt, to gel with his new teammates and to rediscover his form. But he didn't have time. The Manchester United fans were impatient for success.

'We've spent lots of money on great new players,' they argued. 'We have to win the league this season!'

'It's time to shine,' Paul said to himself as he walked out of the tunnel and onto to the Old Trafford pitch. The noise of the crowd only added to his adrenaline. With 70,000 fans cheering his name, it really was the Theatre of Dreams. Paul was a cool character and he never felt nervous, even when the pressure was on. He believed in his own talent and he was determined to win. Today, his usual dyed blond hair was gone; Paul meant business.

From the kick-off, he pushed the team forward with his quick passing and powerful runs. United took the lead through a Chris Smalling header and it gave them the confidence to keep attacking. Leicester just could not cope with the pace and trickery of Jesse

Lingard, Marcus Rashford, and especially Paul. He
was running the show.

As he dribbled forward, he chipped an amazing
pass through to Zlatan Ibrahimović, who chested the
ball down and volleyed just over the bar.

'That would have been the best goal ever!' Paul
said with a big smile on his face. He was really
enjoying himself.

When Paul got the ball on the left, he only had
one thought: shoot. He cut inside and hit a rocket of
a shot. *Booooooooooom!* The ball swerved through
the air. The goalkeeper had no chance but it struck
the post.

'Nearly!' Paul said to himself. 'Next time, I'll score.'

Juan Mata dribbled forward and passed to Paul.
Without taking a touch to control the ball, he flicked
a beautiful pass to Jesse, who flicked the ball into
Juan's path. Juan fired into the net to complete a great
team goal.

'What an unbelievable move!' Marcus shouted as
they all celebrated together.

United's team were on fire and three minutes later,

Marcus made it 3-0. Then just before half-time, Daley Blind swung a corner into the penalty area. Paul used his strength and height to get past his marker and head the ball into the far corner.

Gooooooooooooaaaaaaaaaaaaaalllllllllllllllllllllll!!!!!!!!

Paul finally had his first Manchester United goal and it was an amazing feeling. The supporters expected to see his trademark celebration, 'The Dab', but they would be disappointed. Instead, Paul pointed towards the sky and breathed a sigh of relief. He was finally off the mark, four years after making his club debut, and he was starting to prove his critics wrong.

'Congratulations, that will be the first of many!' Jesse said, giving his friend a big hug.

It was the kind of man-of-the-match performance that Mourinho had broken the world transfer record for. Each time Paul got the ball, every touch was positive and exciting, and the Manchester United fans cheered loudly and hoped for another goal. He was the heart of the team, just as Mourinho had told him to be.

'That's much better!' the manager told him at the

final whistle. 'You're a world-class player and you showed that today.'

Paul was pleased with his display and, most importantly, with the three points from the win. He had returned to Old Trafford dreaming of winning the biggest trophies: the Premier League, the FA Cup and the Champions League. Every victory was a step towards achieving those goals.

'Yes, but I can do even better,' Paul replied, full of confidence.

He was always looking to improve. He had learnt from the best – Patrick Vieira, Zinedine Zidane, Paul Scholes and Andrea Pirlo – and he was still learning from the best. Superstars like Zlatan and Wayne Rooney had lots of experience and tips to share. Paul was ready to do everything possible to be the best midfielder in the world.

He had come a long way from the Renardière estate in France but he was still the same Paul he had always been. He was curious, competitive, gifted, unique, but above all, a born leader and a born winner.

ZINEDINE ZIDANE
HONOURS

Juventus

🏆 Serie A: 1996–97, 1997–98

Real Madrid

🏆 UEFA Champions League: 2001–02

🏆 La Liga: 2002–03

France

🏆 FIFA World Cup: 1998

🏆 UEFA European Football Championship: 2000

Real Madrid

🏆 Ligue 1 Player of the Year: 1996

Ballon d'Or: 1998

FIFA World Cup Final Man of the Match: 1998

- 🏆 FIFA World Player of the Year: 1998, 2000, 2003
- 🏆 French Player of the Year: 1998, 2002
- 🏆 UEFA Euro Player of the Tournament: 2000
- 🏆 Serie A Footballer of the Year: 2001
- 🏆 UEFA Champions League Final Man of the Match: 2002
- 🏆 UEFA Club Footballer of the Year: 2002
- 🏆 UEFA Best European Player of the Past 50 Years: 2004
- 🏆 FIFA World Cup Golden Ball: 2006

ZIDANE

(10) **THE FACTS**

NAME: Zinedine Yazid Zidane

DATE OF BIRTH: 23 June 1972

AGE: 45

PLACE OF BIRTH: Marseille

NATIONALITY: French

BEST FRIEND: Christophe Dugarry

CURRENT CLUB: Real Madrid

POSITION: CAM

THE STATS

Height (cm):	**185**
Club appearances:	**681**
Club goals:	**125**
Club trophies:	**13**
International appearances:	**108**
International goals:	**31**
International trophies:	**2**
Ballon d'Ors:	**1**

★ ★ ★ **HERO RATING: 93** ★ ★ ★

GREATEST MOMENTS

Type and search the web links to see the magic for yourself!

17 AUGUST 1994, FRANCE 2-2 CZECHOSLOVAKIA

https://www.youtube.com/watch?v=7J5hX4VBoOc&t=210s
After choosing to play for France over Algeria, Zinedine made an amazing start to his international career in a friendly against Czechoslovakia. When he came on at half-time, France were losing 2-0 but he scored two late goals, including a header, to save the day. It was a sign of great things to come…

20 OCTOBER 1996,
JUVENTUS 2-0 INTER MILAN

https://www.youtube.com/watch?v=ez32mFd937I

In 1996, Zinedine moved to Italy to join Champions
League winners Juventus. It was a big new challenge
for him but he became an instant star. This was
Zinedine's first goal for the club, a brilliant strike from
the edge of the penalty area against rivals Inter Milan.
Juventus went on to win the Serie A title for two
seasons in a row.

12 JULY 1998,
FRANCE 3-0 BRAZIL

https://www.youtube.com/watch?v=4rMZcpr32n4

This was the night that Zinedine became a national
hero and a world superstar. France had never won the
World Cup until that night in Paris. Ronaldo's Brazil
were the favourites to win but Zinedine stole the show
with two brilliant first-half headers and a stunning
midfield masterclass.

PLAY LIKE YOUR HEROES

THE ZINEDINE ZIDANE 'MARSEILLE ROULETTE'

SEE IT HERE You Tube

https://www.youtube.com/watch?v=u0cusxYv2Lw

STEP 1: Dribble forward gracefully, looking like a king with all the time in the world.

STEP 2: As a defender comes in for the tackle, drag the ball back with your right foot.

STEP 3: It's time to turn away into space. Use your body to shield the ball.

STEP 4: As you spin around in a full circle, use your left foot to drag the ball round with you.

STEP 5: Move the ball back on to your right foot and dribble away with a burst of pace.

STEP 6: If you're not feeling too dizzy, do the Marseille Roulette again on the next defender. It works every time!

TEST YOUR KNOWLEDGE

QUESTIONS

1. Which was the first international tournament that Zinedine watched on TV and what was so special about it?

2. What two things made Zinedine's seventh birthday so amazing?

3. How old was Zinedine when he joined AS Cannes?

4. What was Zinedine given when he scored his first goal for AS Cannes?

5. Who were Zinedine's two favourite teammates at Bordeaux?

6. Zinedine scored on his France debut – true or false?

7. How much did Real Madrid pay for Zinedine in 2001?

8. What shirt number did Zinedine decided to wear at Real Madrid and why?

9. What was Zinedine's last ever professional football match?

10. How many Champions League finals did Zinedine play in?

11. How many international tournament finals did Zinedine play in?

Answers below. . . No cheating!

1. It was the 1982 World Cup and it was special because both of Zinedine's countries were playing - France but also Algeria, where his parents came from. 2. His parents bought him a brand-new pair of Kopa football boots and France won their Euro 84 semi-final against Portugal. 3. 14 4. A brand-new red Renault Clio car 5. Christophe Dugarry and Bixente Lizarazu 6. True – he actually scored twice! 7. £45.8million available 9. The 2006 World Cup Final 10. 3 – 1997, 1998 and 2002 8. 5 because it was the only number between 1 and 11 that was 11. 3 – World Cup 1998, Euro 2000 and World Cup 2006

This summer, your favourite football heroes will pull on their country's colours to go head-to-head for the ultimate prize – the World Cup.

Celebrate by making sure you have six of the best Ultimate Football Heroes, now with limited-edition international covers!

∴ COMING 31ST MAY ∴

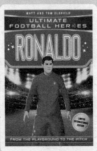

FOLLOW IN THE FOOTSTEPS OF LEGENDS. . .

Bridge the gap between past and present by stepping into the shoes of six classic World Cup heroes and reading their exciting stories – from the playground to the pitch, and to superstardom!

:* COMING 31 ST MAY *: